I'm Sorry,
You Were Saying?

MARTIN STRÖM WITH SARA HULTMAN

I'M SORRY, YOU WERE SAYING?

To Tara and Maria
MARTIN STRÖM

To Elmer and Assar
SARA HULTMAN

"The impact of the practices in this book are truly profound. By training our minds to be more focused, calm, and clear we become more effective at work. But we can also lay a foundation for a more humane world. This book is filled with stories of people who through the practice of mindfulness have become not only more calm and productive, but also kinder and more content with life. It shows how we, by training our minds, can affect change, not only in companies and organizations but also in the communities where we live."

LINDA NORDIN, SECRETARY GENERAL, UNITED NATIONS ASSOCIATION

"What a rich book! A tapestry of different stories and methods skillfully revolves around the often-misconstrued topic of focus. This is a valuable resource for anyone who needs to learn the art of focus at work and in life—which actually includes everyone!"

LINDA BJÖRK, AUTHOR OF INNER BUSINESS, TRAINING YOUR MIND FOR LEADERSHIP SUCCESS

"The impact of living a professional life that is busy, distracted and overly full can be quite distressing and can have a dramatic impact on your effectiveness, your sense of balance and composure. I know first-hand the power of the techniques taught in this book from the corporate mindfulness program we have implemented globally in our law firm. *I'm Sorry, You Were Saying* is filled with research, techniques, and stories of people who have improved the quality of their professional lives through daily mindfulness exercises, and more mindful approaches to common work challenges. I highly recommend it."

MURRAY PATERSON, HEAD OF LEARNING & DEVELOPMENT, GLOBAL LAW-FIRM HERBERT SMITH FREEHILLS

"This book will provide you a clear path to developing a more mindful and effective working life. Through storytelling, science and real case stories you will learn how to enhance your creativity, wellbeing and performance through applying mindfulness to the way you work – and live. Martin Ström is indeed one of the pioneers and experts in bringing mindfulness to the world of work. He generously shares the wealth of experience he has gathered through his work with the CBMT program within Potential Project."

RASMUS HOUGAARD, FOUNDER AND MANAGING DIRECTOR, POTENTIAL PROJECT, AUTHOR OF ONE SECOND AHEAD

"Delighted to see the publication of this book! We are living in a quiet crisis of what is most fundamental to our quality of life: the ability to control our own attention. This book offers helpful, practical tools for reclaiming our basic source of effectiveness and well-being."

JEREMY HUNTER, PHD, FOUNDING DIRECTOR, EXECUTIVE MIND LEADERSHIP INSTITUTE, PETER F DRUCKER GRADUATE SCHOOL OF MANAGEMENT

"Event management has been called out as one of the 5 most stressful occupations. Exposure to the practices in this book have helped my team become more focused, calm and productive. Mindfulness training has lead us to recognize the stress points in our daily interactions with business colleagues as well as in our personal relationships; and adopting some of the ideas highlighted in this book have helped us make small changes that continue to lead to positive results. I recommend this book to anyone who wants to improve their interactions with others.

BARBARA DEANGELIS, HEAD OF EVENT PLANNING FOR A GLOBAL MANAGEMENT CONSULTING FIRM

CONTENTS

1. **TWO MINUTES TO NINE** – *Why mindfulness at work?* ... **15**

2. **HOW TEN MINUTES CHANGED THE LIFE OF A DANISH MARKETING MANAGER** – *The myth of multitasking* **25**

3. **AMANDA BOUNCED OFF THE WALL** – *How to stop being stressed* **45**

4. **WHAT IS MINDFULNESS AND MINDFULNESS TRAINING?** – *Definitions and basic exercises* **63**

5. **WHY ARE YOU WORKING?** – *How the IT manager could really become a leader, the artist found joy in a glue gun, and how to create sustainability for yourself and your organization* **77**

6. **THE CONSULTANT WHO SOUGHT HAPPINESS** – *Productivity – a way to relax* **99**

7. **TRAIN YOUR BRAIN!** – *How mindfulness causes neurological change* **117**

8. **THE JOURNALIST WHO DISCOVERED HER GUT FEELING** – *How mindfulness is related to creativity and innovation* **131**

9. **THE BIRCH TREE THAT CHANGED THE LIFE OF A CEO** – *How the challenges of a leader can be overcome by mindfulness* **147**

10. **CBMT – A MINDFULNESS TRAINING PROGRAM** – *Establishing a habit* **163**

FOREWORD

MY ORGANIZATION, IKEA OF SWEDEN (IOS), is often referred to as the "heart of IKEA". We develop and make the IKEA range available to stores and customers globally. Our company brings together talent from all over the world in an environment of high-paced R&D and extraordinary demands for excellence.

A few years back, Martin Ström was invited to IoS to give a keynote presentation on Corporate Mindfulness. Directly after the presentation I walked up to Martin and asked him how we could incorporate mindfulness training into our organization. I knew immediately and instinctively that this was something from which we would benefit tremendously. What really struck me was the insight that it is possible to create new neurological pathways in the brain, in the same way that you can get in shape physically, learn to play an instrument, or build muscles. Becoming aware of the possibility to train the "attentional muscle" of our brains to gain more focus and awareness was a big eye-opener to me, and many of my staff. We ended up implementing the Corporate Based Mindfulness Training (CBMT) program, which has been running continuously at IoS ever since.

We evaluated the effects of the programs and found a 27% decrease in stress, while the ability to focus increased with 19% and productivity by 7%. Everyone who took part in the program would also recommend it to others. The results of our yearly employee satisfaction surveys also confirm these great results. The participants in the programs reported positive effects on many different levels. For many the most important results were even outside of work, with a greater sense of joy, satisfaction, and general life balance.

IKEA is a highly values-driven company. The Scandinavian way of doing things is in our genetic makeup as an organization. My colleagues are all driven by our vision to create a better everyday life for the many people. At the same time we are all in an ever-changing business environment where focus, attention and awareness is a scarcity. In a global world with cutthroat competition the required pace of innovation is staggering. Companies who have the capacity to harness engagement and extract creativity and energy when it is needed the most will have a competitive advantage. We need to be highly productive and efficient, while at the same time creating innovative, sustainable work cultures. For us, corporate mindfulness has been the way for us to combine such seemingly conflicting goals.

In *I'm Sorry, You Were Saying?* Martin Ström draws on his many years of experience and expertise to demonstrate how mindfulness training can result in greater mental clarity, resiliency and effectiveness. The book, which Martin Ström has written together with author and psychologist Sara Hultman, is bolstered by a strong foundation of research, and presents practical tools that have the power to completely change the way we work. It also contains a plethora of stories from leaders and professionals who have transformed their work experience through mindfulness training. In this book you will find all the mindfulness techniques we have very successfully worked with at IoS in order to provide our people with the tools to perform at the highest level while maintaining balance, focus, and creativity.

Personally the mindfulness training has had a huge impact on my own well-being and my leadership. My focus, attention and awareness as well as my resilience to stress has increased tremendously. I have also realized that there are effects on many levels to be gained from mindfulness training, and some of those effects takes a longer time to manifest. Through the training I find myself and my colleagues also becoming kinder to ourselves and each other. I think that mindfulness holds the potential to shift entire corporate cultures to make them more values driven, more sustainable, and perhaps even more compassionate. We spend a third of our life at work, and companies and corporations have tremendous influence on the world we all share. Mindfulness training is not only about making us as individuals more efficient and less stressed. The real power of mindfulness in the workplace might be to ultimately help create a more peaceful world by transforming the very way organizations operate.

This book contains powerful techniques to train your brain for more focus, balance, and joy. Everyone who wants to flourish while performing at the highest level should read it. But do not expect a quick fix! Expect rather to keep at it for a long time. It is like any type of exercise, if the practice is not continuous and sustained you will not get results. This is also probably the main reason why I would recommend that you to read this book and really put it into practice. It is written to be a practical companion on your journey to implement mindfulness in the way you work, and in life in general. Let it be your guide. And remember: stick with the training!

PÄR STENMARK, MANAGER AT IKEA OF SWEDEN

[...] while the farmer became *exhausted* from his work and the factory worker *bored,* the knowledge worker becomes *worried.*

CHAPTER 1

TWO MINUTES TO NINE

WHY MINDFULNESS AT WORK?

IT'S TWO MINUTES TO NINE. Helen is half running through the open office space, balancing her latte in one hand and the computer in the other, hunting for an empty workstation. All the good spots—the desks at the end, the corners and the lounge-sofa behind lush plants—are already taken. Since the last reorganization, shifting to an activity-based office, everyone tries to get to work before everyone else, minimizing the risk of ending up in the middle of the floor with fellow employees surrounding you 360° and maximizing the chances of sitting next to your friends.

During the extra round through the office, Helen is trying to remember if there is anything in particular on the agenda today. Something is poking at the back of her mind, but she is too caught up in looking for a good spot to pay attention to it. Also, pictures from the morning's battle of getting to school in time keep popping up into her head. Why was she so harsh on Laura—shouting at her 7-year-old—before leaving? Beautiful Laura, with that disappointed face saying goodbye in the schoolyard.

Oh! Helen gives up the search and plunks her stuff down on an empty 360° desk, only two units down from "Loud Ben". Ughh! Opening her laptop, she gets the idea to send a "forgive me" text with a big red heart to Laura. That would lessen her own guilt and smooth things over with Laura. Yes! Helen instantly feels better. While browsing through her e-mail and calendar simultaneously, Helen grabs her phone from her pocket to text Laura. Oh, the calendar shows her that she is free all morning. Great. Helen takes a breather.

She opens up her phone and finishes off her coffee while her fingers automatically click on Instagram. Since there is nothing urgent, except for that report that isn't due until later this afternoon, Helen gives herself a moment to relax and lower her pulse before getting started. So, she swipes through pictures from her friends and, while she's at it, she checks the news on Facebook, too, while keeping one eye on the computer screen. Viber is beeping. And new e-mails have already arrived. Helen scrolls through the subject heading and leaves several of the mails open, intending to answer them later once her desk is clean. Oh, there is one about the conference she should attend. She might as well sign up right now, so she won't forget. The conference's website has an awful lot of information and Helen gets caught up in an interesting article before getting disturbed by Loud Ben laughing on the phone. Looking up, Helen remembers Laura. Maybe she should even buy tickets for the movies tonight to make up for the disastrous morning. Yeah, that will be a nice surprise! When she opens the movie theater website, the internal chat window pops up at the bottom of the screen. It is from the marketing manager saying, "Where are you?" Where are you? Helen repeats blankly to herself. Where am I?

In a flash, Helen suddenly recalls this morning's client meeting. How could she have forgotten? They had pushed it forward to today. The sound on the subway must have been so loud that she hadn't heard the reminder on her phone this morning. Oh no! Helen gets angry with herself for not getting around to syncing her phone's calendar with her computer. What now? She pokes at her cuticles and sends Laura a "text you later," as excuses rush through her head. "I'll be there in five," Helen answers, and then adds "I'm sorry." She grabs her phone and rushes to the elevator. Seven minutes later, as she gets to the meeting Helen's brain goes into overdrive. Panic and guilt pulse through her body and she finds it difficult to focus on the meeting. At one point, the client and the marketing manager look at her expectantly and Helen realizes it is her turn to say something. But, she's gone blank and all she can say is "I'm sorry, you were saying?"

If Helen could read this account, she would probably realize that she was trying to engage in so-called multitasking, instead of focusing on one task at a time, but hindsight is always 20/20.

You may have come across this book because you are in a similar work situation. Perhaps you have experienced a reorganization that resulted in more work, shorter deadlines and undefined tasks. If you are like most others, you are connected and contactable by both PC and your cell phone, at least one of each. You have colleagues, managers and perhaps customers with whom you need to keep in touch and, apart from your core mission, there is a pile of administrative tasks. You are also expected to communicate what you are doing. Meetings, emails and debriefing are recurring items on your agenda. Although you max out your working time, you also feel the requirement to develop. It may be your desire because you want to keep learning and ensure that your organization is at the forefront. You never know, your employment may be determined by a global market over which you have no control, or maybe it disappears in a puff of smoke during the next public procurement.

You probably also feel, just like Helen, that the boundary between work and private life has become blurred. It is perhaps most evident in your Facebook account, where your 539 friends also include colleagues, acquaintances, relatives and half the class from primary school!

All of these factors have contributed to a very complex work situation, which has become the norm for those who have so-called "knowledge worker" jobs.

And, that could have all been fine, if your brain kept developing in the same way. But it is not. Unlike the rapid change that has occurred in the workplace, the human brain has not adapted at the same rate. It is still quite primitive and can only relate to one stream of information at a time, and it goes all too frequently into a stressed state, a flight-or-fight mode (as Helen did, being reminded of the meeting she had forgotten) or, in a less acute version, a wandering mind—where our brains simply can't stay focused on the task at hand—because our attention muscle in the brain is too weak.

In simple terms, one can say that while the farmer became exhausted from his work and the factory worker bored, the knowledge worker becomes worried. Today, mind wandering is the single largest psychological problem in the modern workplace.

Psychologically, one can understand mind-wandering as either an attempt to mentally solve problems in the future, avoid unpleasant emotions in the present or simply the fact that our attention is unconsciously being hijacked by distractions. Since we often do this while we have another task at hand, it is not the best way to complete a physical task while being present with our colleagues or loved ones or to solve a mental problem. Contrary to what we would like to think—that we are the kings of queens of multitasking—we can only focus on

one

thing

at

a

time.

If you've ever tried to unpack the groceries, tend to the kids and do the wash the dishes at the same time, you might have experienced how the ice cream ended up in the cupboard and the underwear in the freezer!

The knowledge worker has a similar challenge. If you attempt to finish writing your emails when your colleague shows up at the door, you may be using 60 percent of your attention on the screen, and 40 percent for listening. The consequence is that your colleague feels uncomfortable and ignored, while you miss essential information and probably forget some of what you were going to write in the e-mail.

It doesn't make you happier either. To think about your Christmas vacation at your desk is more closely tied to negative emotions than focusing on your work, no matter how much you're looking forward to Christmas. In the short-term, it feels like a relief to escape to a pleasurable thought, instead of typing the report that is due, but in the long-term, unresolved tasks pile up, which will now have to be done in less time. The result: more stress and poorer performance.

As the consequences of a fragmented and stressful working life have become more apparent, research efforts to find preventative measures or a cure has escalated. There have been some exciting discoveries about how mindfulness training affects our brain, our health, our efficiency and our mood. In short, one can say that mindfulness training means that you consciously focus your attention, without letting yourself be disturbed by distracting thoughts, feelings and impulses. Examples of how this influence manifests itself are found in each chapter of this book.

There is now intensive worldwide research to identify exactly what happens in our brain when we practice mindfulness. Although people have meditated for 2,500 years—mindfulness exercises originated in Buddhist meditation culture—this is a relatively new field of research in neuroscience. Thus, the results and interpretations of these studies are often characterized by a degree of caution, according to good research practice, until studies demonstrate more sustainable results.

However, what the researchers are in full agreement about—and what is perhaps the most important lesson—is that the brain is far more malleable than previously thought. We can train, restructure and strengthen many brain functions well into old age, similar to how we can build up our biceps at the gym.

An increasing amount of research is being conducted within organizational psychology and related disciplines to see what impact mindfulness training has in the workplace. Although the number of studies to date is limited, there are plenty of individual studies showing how mindfulness increases attention and productivity, and decreases stress and multitasking, which is highly relevant, whether you are employed, a freelancer or a CEO.

In this book, we have accumulated knowledge, research, experience and personal stories from psychologists, knowledge workers and brain researchers, mindfulness instructors and organizational consultants. These people have united mindfulness with working life in different contexts and from different perspectives.

When we started writing the book in 2012, many companies and authorities were curious, but somewhat hesitant to take the plunge. Then, came the "ketchup effect." In Swedish, the "ketchup effect" means that at first there is nothing, even though you keep shaking and shaking the bottle, and then suddenly everything comes out at once. Today, it would be difficult to give the statistics—the number of workplaces where employees and managers spend time on a daily basis taking care of their mind is increasing every day.

And, who wouldn't take the plunge? Especially, when you consider the mentioned and subsequent results—within reach by doing an extremely simple exercise 10 minutes a day—that need no gadgets, just somewhere to sit and a timer, and that everyone can understand and learn in less than 30 minutes.

That is not to say that the training is easy to maintain or a quick fix.

Organizations who have taken the plunge early on have reported:

• Greater productivity
• More effective meetings
• Greater commitment
• Better decision-making and prioritization
• Increased creativity and innovation
• Less sick leave and employee turnover
• Fewer conflicts

On a personal level, the list of results is very long—but these of course benefit the organization as well—so let's stick to the most relevant research related to work life:

• Better sleep
• Greater motivation
• Less stress
• Better relationships
• More joy
• Greater ability to regulate emotions, such as frustration and anger

An inspiring example of mindfulness training can be found at If P&C insurance company in the Danish town of Hvidovre. Since 2009, the department manager, Halldor Machholm, and the staff have been meeting daily for ten minutes in a simple conference room for their morning practice of mindfulness. One year after the inception of this training, 88 percent of the practitioners stated that they experienced increased focus on work tasks, three in four enjoyed their work more, and 65 percent thought that they had become more efficient and productive. More than half also claimed that they were able to handle stress better. In an interview, Machholm says the effects not only benefit the practitioners, but the entire department has changed in a similar way. Here he summarizes what mindfulness has meant for him personally:

"I think that mindfulness is significant in a more fundamental way, to understand the big picture and see what you are doing in context. I notice that I am clear and calm, and able to stop in the middle of everything and experience where I am. If your mind is not calm and focused, you are just fiddling around."

The program that Danish company If P&C uses is called CBMT, Corporate-Based Mindfulness Training. This program forms the basis of most of the exercises in this book. One of the authors (Martin), has conducted the first scientific study in Sweden. Results from the study, which was carried out at an IT company, show that the group of employees who regularly trained in mindfulness experienced an increase in efficiency and productivity by 17 percent, while the perceived stress in the same group decreased by 36 percent. In another study, Martin conducted for a global pharmaceutical company that had completed the CBMT program, the results showed a large reduction of perceived stress at 37 percent. At the same time, there was a 10 percent increase in productivity and efficiency with those who practiced mindfulness. Both of these effects were well above the level of statistical significance, as determined by research practice.

The CBMT program has been developed by an international group of researchers in psychology and neuroscience, as well as by business leaders and mindfulness experts. The program development took six years and was led by the company Potential Project and its Danish founder, Rasmus Hougaard. Among the larger companies that have worked with CBMT are Google, Carlsberg, Sony, Johnson & Johnson, IKEA, Accenture, MasterCard, Microsoft and Nike.

In his best-selling book, *One Second Ahead*, Rasmus Hougaard points out why managing our attention has become such a hard currency for companies and organizations. Without it—without being mindful—he stresses, even the smartest people underperform, due to the fact that their minds wander off unconsciously almost half their waking time. This autopilot behavior is explained by two major short-term behaviors: grasping for things we like and avoiding those we don't like.

What mindfulness practice helps us to do is spotting (and, thereby, avoiding) this "short-term" behavior, instead focusing on the thoughts, decisions and acts that lead us toward our desired goals, often rewarded in a more long-term and sustainable way. With mindfulness training, Hougaard emphasizes, it won´t take you more than about one second to shift from an unconscious automatic reaction to a trigger to a mindfully conscious action (and, thus, the title of the book).

We are aware that the image of mindfulness that we have painted is entirely positive. The fact is that, out of all of the books and reports we managed to plough through (about 50 new studies are published each month), we have not been able to find any risks or negative side effects of practicing mindfulness.

In the worst case scenario, studies have not shown any significant results. That is probably because there are methodological weaknesses in the research, which sometimes makes it difficult to interpret. There are differences in how mindfulness is understood and practiced—few studies use active control groups and sometimes there is a lack of objective measurements. In such cases, it may be difficult to determine the degree to which the results depend on the specific or nonspecific effects of mindfulness training. One research team stated that it is necessary to increase the understanding of mindfulness and mindfulness training, not only how the concept should be interpreted, but also how mindfulness training should be measured and which components should be included in the training. We hope that our book may be a contribution to this direction of thought.

How to use this book

This is not a book that you need to read from cover to cover. It is likely that some of the chapters interest you more than others. Perhaps you are struggling with multitasking and stress, or are looking for ways to increase your capacity for innovation. Then you go to Chapters 2, 3 and 8. In Chapters 4 and 7, we sketch out the concept of mindfulness, as well as describe how the training affects you and your brain. We recommend that you begin the training using the basic exercises on focused and open attention at the end of Chapter 4.

In each chapter, we concentrate on a specific aspect of working life. Research results are interspersed with the voices of people describing how the training has changed their working life and private life. We also provide suggestions for exercises you can try, as well as give you advice and tips on how you can give your work (and life) more meaning, focus and joy.

The exercises from the CBMT program can be found in Chapter 10. If you want to get started right away with your own training, you can start there, but it could facilitate your understanding and motivation if you read the other chapters first.

In the same way as with physical training, the results come with some effort. Research shows that 10-15 minutes a day can produce very good results. It is important, however, that you train regularly.

For the comprehensive development of your workplace, it is desirable for your colleagues and managers to also participate in a mindfulness program. If, for some reason, that does not happen, we advise you to start practicing on your own, or to find a mindfulness group.

When your "attention muscle" starts to grow, this will affect you and your work situation, as well as your colleagues. Exactly how it will affect you remains for you to discover...

Give *100 per cent*, or leave it altogether.

CHAPTER 2

HOW TEN MINUTES CHANGED THE LIFE OF A DANISH MARKETING MANAGER

ABOUT THE MYTH OF MULTITASKING

I was a champion in multitasking. I would have ten emails open simultaneously and be answering some of each. At home, I was proud of the fact that I could start both the washing machine and the dishwasher, while I did a third task – perhaps work. I thought it was a virtue to do everything simultaneously. When I arrived at my first retreat and the leader said that multitasking is the worst thing you can do, I thought, "What?!" I had never thought of it as anything else than obviously a good thing to do.
Gitte Matzen

Gitte Matzen was Marketing Manager for five years at Irma, a grocery chain in Denmark. At the head office in Albertslund, 20 km outside of Copenhagen, she led a marketing group of five people, who organized delivery, customer magazines, advertising campaigns, shop decor and online shopping. Gitte described her job as constantly growing in scope.

The demands of her entire department were increased by a greater organizational complexity in terms of new marketing channels, a growing number of subordinates and more meetings. Her own working hours increased from 40 to 45 hours a week in two years. Given this change, it is a strangely calm voice that reflected on the state of affairs on the other end of the telephone. Calm is also the word that Gitte used several times as she described how she approached all the different tasks—calmly and with focus, using the motto: one thing at a time.

It had not always been like this, however. The beginning of 2011 proved to be difficult. Challenges in her private life created uncertainty about the future, and Gitte tried to fend off the uncertainty and insecurity using the safest thing she had—her job. She was already an appreciated and hard-working manager, and now she stepped on the accelerator even more. This resulted in more and more hours at the office, and when she was at home, mentally she was still at work. "I found solace in my colleagues who appreciated me for what I did. This was the way I used to manage the chaos in my life."

It was in this state that the second test came. The company had hired an advertising agency to launch a new advertising campaign. The lavish ads were post-it notes on which a woman had written a message to her husband. The question was something like: how had they gone wrong in bringing up their son, because now he wanted to do ballet? Would her husband possibly be able to do something quite masculine with the boy to counteract this development?

"It was meant to be funny, of course, but the reaction was huge. Our email server crashed, and we got so much adverse criticism in the media that the CEO had to go on the radio to apologize for the whole campaign. I felt so guilty—I took the blame for everything. People wrote that the person who was behind the campaign should be fired, and that they would never shop at Irma again. I completely lost my way. The place where I had been so successful and safe, no longer existed."

That was when Gitte's boss handed over the contact details of the mindfulness instructor Rasmus Hougaard, who had organized a weekend retreat. Without knowing anything about mindfulness, Gitte grabbed the lifeline and went on the retreat.

24-minute meditation sessions, interspersed with lectures from Friday to Sunday became the turning point in Gitte's life. She described the change as going from the darkness into the light, even if it didn't happen over-night. "It was not like I woke up one morning and everything had changed. It happened slowly, probably a little every day. It is difficult to pinpoint exactly what happened. It was and continues to be a subtle internal change that has occurred gradually. What I have achieved is a newfound sense of peace, and I feel extremely comfortable to be me.

Today, when Gitte is talking about then and now, she is referring to the time before and after learning about mindfulness.

In practice, the training begins in the morning with Gitte walking directly from her bed to sit on her little cushion in a corner of the living room. She switches on her iPod and a voice in the earpiece guides her through a sitting meditation, every morning, for ten minutes.

"I have also tried it for twenty minutes, but it doesn't work. I get up early enough as it is, and sometimes I don't even manage ten minutes." If I don't practice as soon as I get up, it doesn't happen, because everyone in the house wakes up and then everything gets going.

The basic exercise is a breathing meditation in which you practice the ability to be present and concentrated by focusing on your breath. Each week, Gitte adds a mental strategy, which she repeats to herself and cultivates during the exercise. These strategies are how to take different approaches to what is happening—e.g. cultivating patience, having confidence in her ability, or accepting things as they are.

Although Gitte says it is difficult to pinpoint exactly what it is in mindfulness training that is transforming her, she describes a big difference in how she handles problems today compared with two years ago.

"Previously, when problems were building up, I would think about them all the time. As for that campaign—I took the reaction so personally, as though it was me they were criticizing. Now, I'm not so overwhelmed by problems any more. I distance myself from them by keeping calm and focusing instead on what I can do. If it is not possible to do anything, I accept that not everything can be perfect, whether at work or at home."

"I don't manage to keep my distance every day, but I remind myself about it all the time. Acceptance is the attitude that has really given me a sense of freedom. When I remember that, I am able to direct my energy towards things that I can actually do something about, rather than feel anxious or guilty about what went wrong."

Gitte gives examples of such a situation—an employee who chose to stop working because the pressure and stress became too much. "Before burnout became common, we were doing everything we possibly could in a situation. If this had happened a couple of years ago, I would have been guilt-ridden and wondered what more I could have done. Now, instead of beating myself up, I remind myself of everything I've done to try to help. I feel calm about my decision, and this certainty gives me more space to direct all my energy to tune into people and help them do what is important now."

Gitte says that the change has taken place both internally and externally. Outwardly, she is more effective and constructive, and at the same time she does not dwell as much on failures. Gitte is able to get more done, make better decisions, and at the same time she feels safer. She finds it easier to prioritize and only do one thing at a time.

How these changes are related to the fact that she is focusing on her breath ten minutes a day, as well as practicing certain mental strategies, is a question that Gitte cannot answer.

Thoughtfully, she explains that she does not really know what is happening on the cushion, but in light of the definite changes that have taken place, she feels very humble about mindfulness, which has facilitated "more space for clarity and peace." This is evident even when Gitte speaks. She listens carefully to the questions and often begins her answers with "I noted how ...," "I noticed that..." or has a short pause, which seems to give her a moment of reflection. It was not like that in the past. Gitte describes how she often allowed impulses and emotions to control her behavior:

"Emotions can be an asset in my work, but sometimes I have used them too much and jumped straight into things instead of waiting. I'm not talking about a long time. It may only take one or two seconds to regain my self-awareness, by breathing and considering whether I should act in this or that way."

"I have also noticed the difference at home. I used to lose my patience if someone, for example, happened to break a glass. That kind of strong reaction has basically disappeared. Now I react more quietly and have time to think, "Should I get angry or help them to sweep up the broken glass?" When I don't use up energy getting angry, I notice that I have more energy to be with the children instead. Of course, I still lose my temper, but this happens considerably less frequently, since I started doing mindfulness training."

Like many other large companies, the supermarket chain Irma has undergone organizational changes that have increased the pressure on employees. Gitte sees how a greater number of increasingly complex tasks has resulted in the staff trying to do many of them simultaneously. This is what Gitte did as well, and still does sometimes. As we saw, Gitte could have ten emails open at once, trying to answer some of each one. Now, her awareness that the job is done less effectively when trying to keep several balls in the air, helps her try to refrain from that.

Occasionally she doesn't succeed, especially when the inbox is constantly full.

"Sometimes I still have four emails open at the same time, but when I start on the fifth, I notice that I am starting to lose the thread. The difference is that now I am aware of it when it happens. I know it's not good, but I am still wrestling with it. I am getting there!"

Some of the clarity and sense of calm that Gitte feels she has achieved in her role as supervisor, rubs off on her employees.

"I believe that I am able to lead my employees on a more individual basis now. Maybe I did it before too, but now I am very aware to provide the support each one needs. I try to be tolerant and friendly, and it seems to be motivating for them. I have received feedback that they appreciate how I am able to focus on their problems and issues that they bring to me."

Although Gitte is working more hours today than two years ago, she feels less stressed. She says that the calm and focus can last all day. Is there no limit, however, to what you can manage with mindfulness training? Gitte reflects for a moment and then replies:

"I don't know how I would manage if they added 50 per cent more tasks. It probably wouldn't work out—there are clearly limits."

Gitte is very careful to point out that she is not a master of mindfulness. She can be careless, and skip pracitce. She still finds it difficult to "get to the cushion," even though the training is only ten minutes.

"I think that is something that does not come naturally to Westerners like myself. We are constantly on the run and have so many things to do, and all the time know what we should do next. I also believe that we are generally very focused on achieving things that are evident externally, which enables others to tell us how good we are. However, the mindfulness training itself is not difficult. The moment I sit myself down on the cushion, I'm happy."

Gitte rarely mentions that she is engaged in mindfulness. She does not want to be a missionary, but sees her journey as completely private. She does not want to risk getting her mindfulness training challenged or belittled by people who have no understanding.

"This is not a dinner party topic. It can be hard for people to understand. Because I choose not to discuss it, I also avoid hearing the prejudices that exist."

Gitte is the only one who practices mindfulness at her workplace, and it can sometimes make her feel alone. She is philosophical about it. She does not want anyone or any outside influence to affect her training, and draws parallels to running. It may help to join a running club, but if there is no club, that does not need to stop you from running. The athletics club in Gitte's life corresponds to retreats that she attends a few times a year, where she trains in a group with people who have had similar experiences.

"The people I have met through mindfulness are sincere, with open hearts and it is so nice when everything else is so hectic and based on what you are doing. It is a place just to be."

When Gitte thinks back to the situation she was in, more than two years ago, and the journey that followed, she is moved.

"You meet many people in your life, and some of them change you. Rasmus [Hougaard] has definitely changed my life, and I am forever grateful to my boss for putting me in contact with him. I don't know how I would have handled this situation if I had not started with mindfulness. We will never know, but don't paint a perfect picture of me. I can only say that things have happened and I don't want to go back to the dark place I was in two years ago. I am honestly scared of that, and this fear makes me return to the cushion each morning."

THE PERSISTENT MYTH OF MULTITASKING

Like Gitte Matzen, most of our workdays consist of hundreds of different tasks. We rush between meetings, and handle one complex task after another. Emails and texts requiring answers come in—a colleague is waiting and decisions need to be made. There is rarely someone who will help us with time management or getting our priorities right. A common reaction when the information comes in from many directions is that we are trying to address them in parallel, perhaps even simultaneously. We have our mobile phone on silent and answer texts during a meeting. We read the new email while we are talking on the phone. We eat lunch at the computer, and we use "breaks" to check Facebook or the internet news.

The myth that effective staff can juggle ten balls in the air is tenacious, although the cost of multitasking is becoming increasingly known. Despite what we believe, our brains can only attend to one task at a time, and if we are able to be fully present doing one thing at a time, then we become more efficient and productive, and we feel better. The only thing that happens, for example, if we are in a meeting and are already thinking about the next, is that we become anxious, fragmented and stressed.

In a classic study on the effects of multitasking, researchers at Stanford University decided to explore what made people good at performing multiple tasks simultaneously. One of the researchers, Clifford Nass, and his colleagues made a bet about which ability these people excelled in. Nass himself thought it was filtering, that they were experts at filtering out what was irrelevant. A colleague thought it was the ability to switch from one activity to another. A third thought it was the ability to organize information efficiently in the working memory. All researchers were confident that experienced multitaskers would excel in some area.

What they found instead was that there were no positive effects of multitasking at all. People who often did many things at the same time were worse at concentrating and staying focused. They found it difficult to distinguish between important and unimportant information, and had a poorer memory. The Stanford study also showed, paradoxically, that the more a person trained in multitasking, the worse the ability to quickly switch between different tasks. Those who were accustomed to multitasking were, in other words, worse at multitasking! The best multitaskers were those who did not attempt it so much, but typically focused on doing one thing at a time.

While it works quite well to focus our thoughts on one thing while we do something else that is habitual and automated, for example, to have a conversation while walking (as long as we know where we are going, and we don't need to make an effort to find the way), people are not designed to perform two demanding tasks simultaneously. On the contrary, multitasking means that we:

- Slow down
- Lose focus
- Become more stressed
- Lose energy
- Have a lower level of performance
- Feel worse
- Become more easily irritated
- Become less creative.

This result has been confirmed in several experiments since the Stanford study. The scientist Harold Pashler demonstrated that people who had the capacity corresponding to a degree at Harvard University, fell to an 8-year-old's cognitive level when they tried to perform two demanding tasks simultaneously. In another experiment, voluntary participants quickly pressed one or two pedals, depending on whether they heard a low or a high note. When the researchers added another simple physical task, the participants could still exercise the task with about a 20 per cent decrease in performance. However, when they added a simple mental exercise, such as adding 5 and 3, the overall performance decreased by half. The investigation of a severe train accident in the US in 2007 revealed that the driver had sent a text message at exactly the same moment that the train accelerated uncontrollably around a bend.

These examples show how we lose our focus and ability to solve problems when we try to do two or more cognitively demanding tasks simultaneously. Why does this occur? It would be so convenient if we could do everything at once. The short answer is that the brain, specifically the prefrontal cortex, which is the part of the brain that handles complex cognitive processes, is not constructed in that way. It is not that it is a lazy part of the body, but that thought processing is a demanding activity, and the brain's resources are only able to process one section at a time.

For example, if Gitte Matzen is considering whether or not Irma will launch a brand new advertising campaign, this activates the following processes in her brain:

- Understanding a new idea requires that the brain be rebuilt. New ideas are like new cars released into a gigantic network of neural highways and country roads. The problem is that the new cars have a different control system that allows them to try to drive in the field where no cars have previously driven. Therefore, new roads need to be built, and the old ones rebuilt or abandoned in order to be able to connect with the new. Well-known neural pathways transport well-known ideas with little effort, but new ideas require a lot of energy.
- Making decisions about the advertising campaign means that Gitte must locate at least two, but preferably several options in the brain, and choose the best. Each of these options generates a series of questions: how will the campaign take shape? Why? When? Where? At what cost? This takes a large amount of the limited energy reserves because:
- The memory must be activated. Gitte may need to search hundreds of memories from different corners of the brain to find the best evidence for her decision, memories which in turn respond to a series of questions: which campaigns has the company already done? How did they turn out? Why was that? What are the competitors doing? How did it work? What is in fashion? What is needed right now? What does the customer need? What does the world need?
- In addition, Gitte needs to memorize new knowledge. In order to even be able to consider the best way to carry out the idea, Gitte's working memory needs to be in such good shape that she manages to keep her

attention on the new information long enough for it to be transferred into her long-term memory.

• While Gitte is going through the process of choosing the best idea, she needs to distance herself from internal distractions (irrelevant thoughts that demand attention) and external distractions (phone calls, emails, meetings and spontaneous questions from colleagues). This in itself is an activity requiring resources.

All of these mental processes are activated when you solve a single cognitive task, even if you are not using them all at once. They are more like a series of events that are activated manually. Each part is fighting for its piece of your limited mental resources, so you need to be extremely careful how you utilize these resources, otherwise there isn't enough to go around.

David E. Meyer, a professor at the University of Michigan, explains that for people to allocate their resources in the most effective way, they need an executive control function, the CEO of the brain, which can monitor every behavioural aspect—perception, thinking and action—so that the allocation of resources is sustainable.

The executive control consists of two parts, according to Meyer. The first is to switch between different objectives—to decide which goal you want to work towards at the moment. The second part involves activating certain internal "rules" in the working memory in order to handle a particular activity, thus disabling other rules.

No matter what control you use, you lose time and energy when you switch targets and thus have to switch from one task to the next. The more complex and new the task, the longer it takes for the brain to activate the rules in order to deal with the "new" task. Switching back and forth between tasks can, therefore, be a way of unnecessarily wasting energy. In extreme cases, it can also be life-threatening, as shown by the example of the train driver above.

However, it is also here, via the brain's CEO, that we have our chance to rise to the challenge of resisting multitasking. By strengthening the CEO function, you can teach yourself not only to change tasks more easily without losing too much energy, but also to keep your attention longer on the task that lies ahead of you. There are several external strategies that can facilitate the brain's CEO to save energy, but because this book focuses on mindfulness, we choose to develop this aspect.

There have been several studies on how mindfulness affects the ability to handle cognitively demanding tasks. One study was carried out by the computer scientist David Levy, together with his colleagues at the University of Arizona, involving three groups of HR specialists.

The mindfulness training that was conducted in one group, dealt with focused attention, and stressed the importance of:

1. The ability to deliberately focus and then broaden the attention and rest your attention on the present moment or the current task.
2. The flexibility to consciously shift attention from one task to another.
3. The ability to develop the awareness of not only the breath, but also the body and other objects.

Mindfulness training was provided for eight weeks. Participants met with an instructor for two hours each week and trained on their own between sessions.

The second group received training in relaxation techniques for eight weeks. The third group did not receive any training at all.

The tests were designed to simulate common tasks on a normal working day: participants used phones, a calendar, email, instant messaging and word processing programs. All tests were designed to be strenuous and stressful.

The results showed that participants in the mindfulness group experienced less stress and fewer negative emotions after eight weeks. In addition, they were less distracted while they worked, and changed tasks less frequently. They also allowed more time for each task. In other words, they devoted themselves less to multitasking.

These results were not found in either of the other two groups. The capacity for memory was strengthened in both the mindfulness and relaxation group.

Exercises in mindfulness thus strengthen the ability to better resist the impulse to do several things simultaneously. By drawing your attention again and again to a conscious goal, you strengthen the brain's CEO function. This ensures that the brain's limited mental resources are able to be maximized. The brain will not become overworked, and you will not feel as though your attention is divided.

START MONOTASKING WITH TWO RULES FOR MENTAL EFFICIENCY

In addition to the official mindfulness-traing that Gitte Matzen does for 10 minutes each morning (introduced in chapter 4) there are two rules for mental efficiency in the Corporate Based Mindfulness Training-program, that can help us to resist multitasking. These rules are based on the two basic forms or minfulness: directed and open attention.

Rule 1: Focus on what you choose

Research has shown that directed attention makes us more efficient and productive, while increasing our psychological well-being. A focused mind does not engage in multitasking, but is 100 per cent absorbed in what you choose as the subject of your attention. You have probably discovered, however, that it is not that simple to keep your focus on what you choose— quite quickly your attention wanders away to other thoughts. However, focus can be improved, which can be seen later in this book.

Imagine that you take the two basic instructions of focus training with you to work: focus on what you choose, and let go of all distractions. Imagine that you are sitting at work on a Monday morning. You have set aside an hour to finish writing that important report. The deadline is fast approaching. As you sit in an open office, you will soon be distracted by a conversation between two colleagues. Their conversation is really interesting, but as you follow rule number 1, you deliberately let go of this distraction as soon as you notice that you have become distracted. Instead, you return your attention to the report.

Some minutes later, you will suddenly think of the dinner party you are invited to that evening. You begin to wonder if you should take a gift and what to wear. You have, in other words, distracted yourself by your own thoughts. However, as soon as you discover that you have been distracted, you return your attention to the report, since it is the anchor for your attention, and you are following rule number 1.

You continue to work in a focused manner, and do not allow your attention to be split by distractions. Suddenly, your boss rushes in. She is as white as a sheet, and tells you that something has happened, which plunges the entire department into an acute crisis. She needs your help immediately to resolve the situation. However, because you have read in this book about the importance of not allowing yourself to be distracted, you continue to follow rule number 1. You ask your boss to kindly wait, and simply return your attention to the report. The following day, you are fired.

Obviously, rule 1 has its limitations. You can follow it for more than 90 per cent of the time at work, but you also need rule number 2.

Rule 2: Consciously choose your distractions

Rule number 2 deals with the practice of being aware of the thoughts and distractions that arise, but without engaging in them. With the help of open attention, you can note when something comes up that is actually more worthy of your focus than what you have chosen for the moment.

An organization cannot function if employees become introverted and closed off. Focus is necessary, but without open attention, energy, productivity and joy can turn into suffering. Rule number 2 ensures that you can work in a focused manner, but at the same time are open to internal and external stimuli. In this way, you pay attention to both a changing reality around you and the creative thoughts that are worth paying attention to.

In the training of open attention (see Chapter 4), you let the distractions become the anchor for your attention. This is also the reasonable response when the boss comes and asks for help. You weigh up that this is more important than the report you are writing and, therefore, consciously move your attention there.

You can let go of at least 90 per cent of all distractions. Then, there is the 10 per cent that you need to consider moving your attention to, because for various reasons they are important or relevant. Directed attention (rule 1) helps you remain doing the tasks you choose. Open attention (rule 2) helps you to change the focus of your attention when it is important to do so.

The ability to evaluate which distractions you should drop and which ones you should follow is something you can significantly strengthen through mindfulness training. In the beginning, we only notice distractions when we have already allowed ourselves to be "kidnapped" by them, and are deeply involved in them. However, with practice, you can catch a distracting thought even before it has taken shape. This ability is something that characterizes a highly effective mind.

Rule number 2 says: "Consciously choose your distractions." There are three ways to react when you choose consciously:

1. You choose not to be distracted, but let go of it.
2. You note the distraction, but choose not to get involved in it right now. If a colleague asks for help, you might say that you can do that in five minutes' time. If you think of something important, you might write it down in order to come back to it later. Then, complete what you were doing with full focus.
3. You choose the distraction fully and make it your new subject of focus, as long as it lasts. What is now crucial is that you completely let go of what you were doing. Your focus subject has now become a distraction—and if the thoughts wander back, then remember rule number 1.

The two rules can be formulated even more simply. When you write an email, use 100 per cent of your attention, or don't write it at all. When you are with someone, be 100 per cent present or don't engage with them at all. Do what you do 100 per cent or leave it altogether.

The key is not to try doing two things mentally at once. As soon as you try to do that, you will be less effective, create more stress and make more mistakes. You lose perspective regarding what is important and a priority. Additionally, you will have less empathy and your social interactions will become shallower and less meaningful. The more you exercise your brain in divided attention, the more split you will feel.

This doesn't mean that you can't keep many balls in the air. Imagine a skilled juggler who has seven balls in the air simultaneously. If this is to succeed, he really needs to focus on one thing at a time. Catch a ball, throw it. Catch the next ball, throw it. The other balls will handle themselves in the meantime. If the juggler moves his attention to a ball other than the one that has just been caught or thrown away, he would drop them all.

The more you train your attention, the better you become at keeping your focus on one thing at a time, and at the same time know when it is time to shift your attention to something else. This saves you time and energy and maintains your inner balance.

Other advice

Become aware of when you are multitasking

It all starts with awareness. Pay attention to what you are doing! When you catch yourself trying to do two things that are cognitively demanding at the same time, drop one task.

TIPS

Gitte's advice

1: Listen actively

If a colleague comes into the office with a question, turn away from your computer and look at the person, or ask them to come in and sit by the desk. Listen actively, respond and relate to the person in question, instead of keeping an eye out for emails.

2: Write a note

If you notice that a distracting thought prevents your focus on the subject you are attending to, write a post-it note, so you can leave the distraction for now, and instead be present where you are. The memo reminds you to take care of the task at a more convenient time.

3: Acceptance

Forgive yourself because you are not a master of mindfulness. Do the exercises anyway. Practice and patience are the only way to achieve change.

Save energy 1

Normally, you have the greatest mental capacity in the morning after a good night's rest. As the brain needs to be alert in order to sort through information, plan the day, prioritize and review problems; it is a good idea to make that the first thing you do at work. Turn off the mobile phone, give yourself five minutes and take control of the day. Start with what feels most difficult. It is probably the task that requires the greatest mental capacity.

Save energy 2

Try alternating cognitively demanding tasks with simple routine tasks. This will give your brain a rest.

Save energy 3

The more you practice a skill, the less effort required to perform it. Mastering keyboard shortcuts and grammar allows you to put more energy into the content of your writing.

In a similar way, with mindfulness training, you will save your mental resources for when you really need them.

Mindful multitasking

If you must engage in multitasking, try combining a cognitive task with a more automated behavior, such as discussing work while you walk.

Trust your brain

If the brain is not under stress, it will remember the most important thing. Trust that it will do that and do not worry that you'll miss something, at least not the most important thing. Maybe you don't even need to write a note?

Work Culture

Create a work culture where colleagues respect each other's need to focus. Write a note on your desk to show when you do or do not want to be disturbed—just like on a hotel door.

Open or closed rooms

Open plan offices make high demands on how we manage to focus our own attention and respect others. It has been shown that open plan offices generally contribute to improved communication and more effective cooperation within and between teams, but it also increases the risk of low individual performance. Unnecessary information from others can affect your cognitive processes negatively in terms of reduced efficiency and increased stress. One study found that individuals with more complex tasks performed better in their own room, while simpler and more repetitive tasks were performed better in the presence of others.

Email and texts

If you are thinking more about what is in the text message that just came in on your mobile than what your colleague is saying in front of you, then it is probably a good idea to turn off the notification signal or vibration function. You can decide how often to check texts and emails. You can devote some time a few times a day to communicate via text and email, for example, morning, lunch, late afternoon. This will work better if you notify those around you of your policy. You can also add an auto reply to emails with a request to call when it is urgent.

Additionally, you can remind yourself that you probably will not have any time for other things if you try to empty your inbox as soon as possible—on the contrary. Rapid response encourages the sender to write more often, and the amount of messages in your inbox will increase the faster you answer all of them. Instead, choose which emails are important and urgent, which ones can wait until later, and which you may not even need to answer.

Facebook, Twitter, blogs

Make a conscious choice about which social media you want to be a part of, and set aside time for this. Be aware that this participation, as well as many work tasks, take away part of your overall mental capacity.

Let your mind rest

A study at the University of London found that constant emailing and texting lowered the IQ of the participants by about 10 points (5 for women and 15 for men). The results have been discussed, but regardless of IQ, it is a fact that the ability to solve problems is lowered when the brain is tired.

Therefore, let the brain rest properly when you "take a break." The alternative to texts and emailing is to get in touch with your physical senses—take a few deep breaths, deliberately walk slowly to the tap and pay attention to what you see and hear on the way. And, when you drink, taste the water!

To do one thing at a time, with *focus* and *awareness* is not stressful in itself.

CHAPTER 3

AMANDA BOUNCED OFF THE WALL

HOW TO STOP BEING STRESSED

One of the symptoms of an approaching nervous breakdown is the belief that one's work is terribly important.
Bertrand Russel

WHEN SIRI URGES THE CHILDREN to put on their shoes and jackets at 7:55 a.m., because it's time to go to school and work, 7-year-old Hector asks, "Are you stressed, mum?" If she has a tight feeling in her throat, tension in her body, with her mind already on the job, Siri would probably respond, "Not now!"

Of course, she should have replied, "Absolutely," because it is true that she is stressed. Her brain is in overdrive, her cortisol levels are high and her thoughts propel her into panic mode. By this stage, Siri can't cope with listening to Hector, or going through the list she has in her head of the things she needs to take with her. She grabs what she can find on her way out the door, snaps at her son, only to realize she has forgotten some things. Hector is dressed, standing at the gate, and counting silently to three as Siri returns three times to retrieve the things she has forgotten, before they finally manage to leave for school.

If Siri would have managed to regain control over her attention at that time, for example by becoming conscious of her breath, she would have been able to pick up the laptop cable, handbag, gym bag, mobile, homework and fruit just as quickly, but more efficiently. She also would have been able to hear Hector's question and been able to answer truthfully, "No, but we need to leave now, so you don't miss assembly at school."

Stress is the reaction of the body and the brain to our inner and outer world, to perceived or actual demands. We can't always influence the outer "stressful" situation, but we can do a lot about our inner reactions. It is crucial for most of us today to find a way to manage stress.

Stress has become an endemic disease, and it is now the main cause of sick leave. Previously, most parents working full-time with young children were at risk, which they still are, but now an increasing number of younger people without families also suffer from stress. And considering the changes of modern worklife, it is not so hard to see why. Just imagine a typical office environment in the 1970s. A person is sitting at a typewriter next to a telephone plugged into the wall. The clock on the wall is ticking, and the coffee machine is simmering. The fax machine in the hall is buzzing. Occasionally. The secretary is on top of things, taking care that the information reaches the right person.

Put that image next to a current snapshot: an activity-based open-plan office, with a person in front of two or three computer screens filled with text, graphs and images. A mobile phone and a tablet are nearby on the desk. The amount of information a knowledge worker is expected to relate to each week far exceeds that which the corresponding person encountered just a few decades ago.

Rasmus Hougaard, who is the founder of the CBMT program, which is the basis of many exercises in this book, uses the acronym PAID to describe the situation most knowledge workers are in today:

- **P:** *pressure.* Pressure is increasing all the time. We are expected to perform more and more, and the amount of work always seems to be greater than the time available to complete it. As soon as one task is finished, the next is waiting.
- **A:** *always on.* The advent of IT means that we are always connected, always switched on. Through computers and smart phones, we have access to work anytime, anywhere. The manager of a large company described how she used to wake up at night and couldn't stop thinking about work. Her solution was to get up and work for an hour to free herself from her thoughts and worries about deadlines and important tasks.

- **I:** *information overload.* We are bombarded by information from all sides. This is information that we have to peruse, sort and prioritize. Imagine a typical office environment in the 1970s:
- **D:** *distractions*—which is what is the most problematic—distractions. Not only is the pressure increasing, we are never disconnected from work and the amount of information we are expected to relate to grows exponentially, but we are also constantly interrupted by distractions. As we discussed in the chapter on multitasking, both internal and external distractions mean that we rarely manage to stay on the same task for more than a few moments or minutes. This scattering of our attention is the greatest contributor to stress.

It can be said that stress occurs when we feel that the PAID factors above go beyond our capacity to cope with them.

There are always two things you can do to reduce the experience of stress. The first is to change the external conditions, such as:

- Creating the best possible routines and structures at work
- Hire enough people to handle all tasks
- Have good IT support
- Take regular breaks and attend fitness classes held in the workplace
- Have competent and empathetic managers.

However, no matter how much the external conditions change, there will always be demands, problems and challenges to meet and overcome. Unfortunately, these requirements only increase. This brings us to the second change you can make, namely to train the mind to function better in a stressful environment. This is where mindfulness comes in. Hans Selye, a physician and pioneer in stress research said already in the middle of the last century: "It's not stress that kills us, it is our reaction to it."

Imagine that you are sitting at work and have to write an important report. The deadline is in about two hours. If you work on the report with full focus and presence, you will not experience stress. However, imagine if you start thinking about what will happen if the report is not ready in time. In your mind, you can see the boss and hear how she is chastising you. This thought loop continues and develops into a one-dimensional disaster scenario: if your boss is unhappy, you might lose your job—then what will happen to the summer house, the mortgage and the trip to Thailand?

Since the brain can't distinguish between real and imaginary threats, the sympathetic nervous system is now kicking in. The body goes into stress mode, and adrenaline and cortisol are released. These stress hormones interrupt contact with the front part of the brain, which is the very part you need to write the report—the part that could give you stability, clarity and awareness. The stress response is now in full swing.

In other words, it is not writing the report, or only having two hours to do it that constitute your stress. The stress is actually borne from your distracting thoughts.

You can radically reduce the experience of stress by training your brain's capacity for directed attention and increasing your awareness. This has been identified in numerous studies that have measured differing abilities to handle external stress. There is a huge variation in this ability. The brain's stress reaction in people who are able to keep their attention on a task without being distracted by other thoughts, is not activated to the same extent as in people who are easily drawn in by external influences (regardless of the external stressors).

Brain researcher Richard J. Davidson interprets the variation in the reaction patterns that people have to stress according to different personality styles. In his book, *The Emotional Life of your Brain* he puts forward the hypothesis that our personality is made up of six basic emotional styles. One of these emotional styles is resilience, which is how quickly you can recover from the onslaught of stress. Davidson has seen that some people return very quickly to their normal resting state, even if they initially suffered a stress reaction, while others get stuck in a wound-up state for a long time. Even if we have different ways of reacting to stress, we don't need to be victims of our different styles. Davidson suggests that mindfulness training strengthens our ability to recover quicker from the stress reaction and return to the baseline state. In some cases, even the initial stress response can be bypassed, but he says that this reaction is stronger and more difficult to influence. Instead of this, he refers to the fact that we can train and improve our resilience, which is the key to building up resistance to stress.

Amishi Jha, a professor of psychology at the University of Miami, raises the discussion about mindfulness and stress to another level. Jha says that stress is, in fact, the racing thoughts, i.e. that thoughts are unconsciously pulled away by distractions.

To elaborate on the hypothesis, she returns to the definition of mindfulness, as formulated by the mindfulness pioneer and doctor Jon Kabat-Zinn, "paying attention in a particular way on purpose in the present moment non-judgmentally." Jha analyses the definition:

1. "Paying attention... in the present moment..."
Imagine that your attention functions like a flashlight that you can consciously direct at will. When you are stressed or depressed, the flashlight moves around in a way that is not useful. It is shining constantly on negative thoughts and it feels like you can't control it. However, if you practice directing your attention, so that in every moment you manage to point the flashlight on the things you want, then the negative feelings will fade away.
2. "...in a particular way..."
This is a hypothesis that you can develop an awareness of what you are experiencing in the moment, i.e. the quality of knowing where you are mentally. What is happening right now? Are you sitting here in the chair, or is your mind somewhere else? Without this awareness, you can't focus your attention on what you want.
3. "...non-judgmentally."
This is about the value-laden emotional meaning we ascribe to phenomena, which is also something you can take control of. If something happens and you say. "This is the worst thing that could ever happen," it is the interpretation you give to the incident. However, if you interpret it differently, e.g. "this is the best thing that could happen" or "this is happening as the result of...," these different interpretations will affect how you relate emotionally to your environment.

These are the core mental functions that can be trained with the help of mindfulness, but Jha clarifies that a fourth point is also important—attention has a limited capacity. That means, if you're wasting your attention by directing it towards something that is not effective, then the brain does not have enough energy to direct it to where you want. Amishi Jha explains:

"I have noticed that people who suffer from stress deplete this capacity by their habitual behavior, in which their attention jumps around in all directions, and their energy to control it has been expended. It is the same with consciousness. If we don't have the ability to discern what we are actually experiencing in our feelings, thoughts and behavior, we will not be able to act with mindfulness, but will react using the same habitually stressed autopilot. It is the same with evaluation. When we consider and look for alternative interpretations, this depletes the limited mental resources of the brain. However, when the resources have been used up, this is hard to do."

STRESS AS A SURVIVAL FUNCTION

From a survival point of view, stress is necessary. If we don't experience acute stress when someone pulls a knife on us, we have a significantly worse chance of survival. Fight or flight is, therefore, a natural and functional response to a real threat. If a man threatens you with a gun, your body will take care of your response in the best way. If you are weak, you might stand very still, and if you're fast, you run away.

The problem arises when we activate the stress response at the wrong time, i.e. if you trigger the stress response when the manager's phone number shows up on the mobile, or get upset about tomorrow's meeting as you lie in bed at night. When this happens, the body has perceived false alarms as true, and feelings of panic trigger unpleasant thoughts that pull you away. As an isolated occurrence, this reaction is not dangerous for your health, but if you often interpret the false alarms as true and respond to any external stressor in overdrive, then your limited resources will soon run out. Your cortisol and adrenaline levels will remain high, and eventually drain the immune system. In the long run, the working memory deteriorates, sleep disorders occur, with the possible onset of a panic disorder and/or depression—the most common symptoms of prolonged stress.

Marianne Siegborn, behavioural therapist and mindfulness instructor has worked with stress problems both proactively and in rehabilitation in Swedish workplaces. She describes a development where both external and internal stressors have increased:

"We know that stress in itself is not dangerous, but that the cutbacks that occurred during the last decades, with greater responsibility, more tasks and fewer opportunities for recovery, is dangerous. We know that natural breaks are disappearing, which is dangerous. Meetings are scheduled in such tight proximity to each other, with neither time to consolidate the previous meeting, nor time to prepare for the next one, which also makes the meetings fairly ineffective. Instead of standing and brewing a pot of coffee while talking about things that may not be directly related to the job, you are expected to fill your coffee cup at the machine and take it back to your desk to continue working. This time together is extremely important, when you can chat about what is happening and experience a feeling of community. You feel mentally relaxed and part of the greater whole."

"Working life has come to contain very complex structures where you have to manage both external and internal stress. In a large organization, you will meet both angry customers, and frustrated colleagues, while dealing with the financial framework imposed on you from above. Additionally, your own performance expectations cause internal stress. What surprises me is that, although we know so much about how stress works nowadays—that it decreases efficiency and results in poor health—workplaces still continue to increase the pressure and reorganize in a way that does not take this knowledge into account. I have seen so many organizations that do not consider long-term effects."

Marianne Siegborn sees middle managers as a particularly vulnerable group, with many demands from several directions. They have a limited mandate, many people to relate to and often have days full of meetings with several different departments.

"You can have a telephone meeting with the CEO who is in Holland, and then instantly go to a production meeting elsewhere. You need to travel to meet with your counterparts in Germany and Denmark, and you are also expected to manage your tasks at the office. This causes stress to many people. There are many meetings that go for several hours without a break, which makes them very inefficient. We know you can be really present and perform at a high level for about 20-25 minutes, then the brain needs rest.

To reduce the stress-inducing factors at work, Marianne Siegborn says that all levels in the organization need to be made aware of internal and external stressors. What usually happens is that an employee or manager who suffers from fatigue is sent off on individual stress treatment. Afterwards, the unstressed person returns to the stressful workplace. It may be possible for participants to sustainably change their inner attitude on an individual level, but she emphasizes that it is necessary for the whole organization to embrace collective change, in order to bring down the stress statistics. She says it doesn't even have to cost any money, since mindfulness not only makes people healthier, but also more effective.

"What would happen if a simple change were made, such as to re-instate breaks and time for reflection, preparation and rest? What would happen if we were recognized for what we actually achieve, instead of focusing on problems? I see mindfulness as a necessary approach in the current work environment, both for life in general and the revving-up process leading to stress. Mindfulness is really necessary for people to be able to continue in the long term."

HOW AMANDA RECOVERED FROM STRESS

Amanda has completed a stress reduction course. We meet at lunchtime in a busy coffee shop in central Stockholm. During the interview, different people ask to share our table. Each time Amanda declines in a friendly manner, with reference to the interview, and each time she picks up the thread exactly where we were, adding that they can come back if there is no other place. Two years ago, Amanda may have reacted with a snide comment instead. "I was very emotional, and it wasn't pleasant for people around me."

Two years ago, there was a re-organization of the large government agency where Amanda was working as a controller. It was the beginning of the outer and inner stress that was to dominate her life over the course of a whole year. Amanda's department grew from three to eleven employees, a colleague became manager and from one day to the next, the group started working in a different way. New tasks were distributed, the roles became blurred and Amanda was asked to take over a whole new area of work. "It was unclear what that meant, but it sounded interesting. I felt flattered and accepted," she explained.

Amanda kept going as best she could. She was at work between 9 a.m. and 8 p.m. and then continued working at home for a few more hours. After three or four months, she noticed that despite all the effort she put in, she couldn't manage everything. Dizziness, chest pressure, forgetfulness and negative thoughts began to increase and soon she was tired, no matter how much she slept. Six months later, Amanda was on sick leave.

Amanda believed the reason she could push herself so hard for eight or nine months was due to being flattered by the offer of greater responsibility, as well as loyalty towards her employer. "I wanted to do a good job. Everyone else had just as much to do. So I thought, if I don't do it, some other poor wretch will have to."

Afterwards, Amanda wondered what she could have done differently, but concluded that she probably did everything possible. "I told my supervisors several times and said, 'No, stop, hire more people'. So it wasn't that I couldn't say no, but at some stage, I began to think that I have to start taking care of myself. Now I think that this was good for me, because I met a doctor who gave me the opportunity to take part in a course on mindfulness. At first I was very skeptical. I thought it was just a trend that you do for a while, and then it runs out of steam."

Amanda went home and rested for two months. After that, she began the mindfulness course, initially with a lot of resistance. "You'd sit there in a group and talk about private things. I can't manage this, I thought. I felt introverted, sitting there revealing things in front of people I did not know! 'How does your body feel?' was a question they might ask. I didn't know—I couldn't find words to describe the feelings that I experienced, I don't think I was in contact with them."

Her strategy often was to wait until the end, until everyone else had said something. Amanda laughs at the memory. "I always said something. I remember that I tried to see it as an exercise in not being anti-social, because when I was stressed, I became extremely withdrawn."

In the beginning, Amanda also felt dizzy when she was training mindfulness. Yet, she persisted and set aside the time prescribed by the program. The dizziness disappeared, and after four or five weeks, she noticed a change. "I felt calmer overall. My body relaxed in a new way. It was great to start thinking along these lines, and slowly decrease the tempo. The focus training helped most of all."

Since the course, Amanda has continued training on her own, at first sporadically and then more regularly. The habit has been established for one year, and Amanda sits down at home several times a week to practice focusing on the breath for 10-40 minutes.

In addition, to the seated practices, mindfulness training involves observing and increasing the awareness of thoughts, feelings and behavior in everyday life, and explores the non-judgmental attitudes of acceptance and curiosity. This awareness has changed Amanda's way of being in a profound way.

"I like this way of thinking. I think I need it. Previously, I tended to make many value judgments about things, and it was very important for me to always give my point of view about everything. I could be very cynical and sarcastic, so it was often an argument or confrontation. Now I can listen, wait and reflect. I may say nothing at all. I let it be, while I think about what the person really said, then it won't be an automatic reaction where someone speaks and gets upset. It becomes calmer and more reasonable. At the same time, I feel that I am more open towards colleagues, both personally and when dealing with work. We discuss more, we have a more open dialogue about how we're doing and I don't just sit on the side-lines. However, I still go off sometimes, and afterwards I think that I should have been able to handle the situation differently. I have a lot of training left ..."

Amanda hopes and believes that the body awareness she has developed with the help of mindfulness, will immunize her against getting stressed again. Now she notices if there is anxiety and restlessness in the body, and when that happens, she listens to the signals.

"When I feel restless, I only need to sit down for ten minutes until I notice that my breathing and pulse slow down, and the body becomes calm. Then it feels like my emotions are balanced again."

The external stressors are still present on the whole. As a controller, you have a deadline every month, which requires being on the ball. What Amanda believes has changed is the ability to return quickly to normal mode, instead of continuing to rev up.

Other aspects of awareness include how present and focused Amanda perceives herself to be at work. She checks these aspects on a daily basis.

– I am careful not to float away in thought, or do several things at once. I try to focus on what I am doing, one thing at a time. It may only be my boss who notices this, but he says that I have become more relaxed. Before I became ill, I tried to squeeze in everything that came my way, but now I say, "No, I don't have time for this." or "No, I won't do that."

So far, it has worked to speak up, says Amanda, and takes a bite of the pastry, that lasts for the whole interview.

"I've become so aware of all this. Another very important aspect is the relationships with managers and colleagues, and how we talk to each other. We're talking everywhere, in meetings, in the corridor and at coffee, but I have begun to notice that people often don't really understand what the other person is saying, or that they have their thoughts elsewhere. Our attention is divided. It's something I really think about now. When I am talking with someone, I'm aware of that person. I didn't do that before— then I could sit and talk to someone, write something else, and think of a third thing."

"Now, there are plans for a further reorganization soon, but despite the dark place Amanda ended up in last time, she takes this new information in her stride."

"We'll see how it goes. I don't know if it's because I've a different way of thinking overall, but ... it will be interesting to see how it affects me this time."

TEN MINUTES A DAY

MBSR (*Mindfulness-Based Stress Reduction*) is a program that has been developed by Jon Kabat-Zinn for people with long-term stress problems. It is quite extensive and can be difficult, or in many cases impossible, to be implemented in the work place. For someone who has already suffered severe stress problems and is currently in the rehabilitation phase, it may be appropriate for them to take part in MBSR, but for most people it is too big of a time commitment. Moreover, not everyone is comfortable with the therapeutic elements that require openness to discuss their own mood at depth with the group. For a workplace and, especially, when it comes to introducing mindfulness training in large groups, there are other programs that are more suitable.

What is interesting, however, is that small "doses," such as only ten minutes a day has been shown to have major effects on stress. As we mentioned in the introductory chapter, the experience of stress in an IT company fell by 37 per cent after ten minutes of mindfulness training per day during a 9 week program. One of the participants reported that he basically no longer felt stressed after the program, even though the actual workload was somewhat greater than before. He attributed this to an increased ability to relate more objectively to his own thoughts, as well as an improved ability to maintain focus on what is important in the moment. Another participant said that she was sleeping more soundly since doing mindfulness training, because she had learnt how to stop thinking about work. She also experienced less stress, which was a consequence of improving her concentration and memory, and being able to prioritize better.

...or one second

An important component that reduces stress is that we become aware of our thoughts and emotional responses at an early stage. Rasmus Hougaard, who has been mentioned several times, described one of his clients, Jakob, the manager of a large bank. Jakob came to Rasmus for help with his work situation, which he felt was becoming increasingly stressful and unsustainable. After Jakob had been practicing mindfulness every day for four months, Rasmus asked what the program had done for him. "One second," replied Jakob. "That doesn't sound like very much," thought Rasmus. However, Jakob explained that "a second," meant that the training had made it possible for him to be one second ahead of his thoughts and feelings.

Earlier, in most situations, he had been reactive and on autopilot, which was usually controlled by his negative feelings. Now, with mindfulness training, he has a space that is perhaps not much longer than a second, in which he can choose how he would like to act instead of react—one second, which gives him time to observe his reactions, emotions, thoughts and interpretations. "Nowadays, I am one second ahead all the time," he said, "and it has changed everything. I don't feel stressed out anymore, although I still have just as much to do."

How mindfulness affects stress

Mindfulness:

- Strengthens your ability to focus your attention on the task that you are doing and to let go of thoughts of the past and the future. To do one thing at a time, with focus and presence, is not stressful in itself. What is stressful, is all the thoughts about how it should be, all the future tasks, and what people will think about the result.
- Makes it possible to develop greater attention to and awareness of signals from the body. If you are early enough, you can catch the signs of when you start to tighten up and breathe more shallowly, and you can take a "mindful" break.
- Trains your ability to focus and concentrate in a way that does not require effort. We are so used to expending energy to concentrate on something. We focus and create tension, then afterwards we are wrung out. When you practice mindfulness, you discover that it's possible to be totally concentrated without any effort.
- Provides increased resilience. If you react strongly to something, you will be able to swing back to "baseline," your normal mode, more quickly.
- Increases your ability to take a different perspective, improves your capacity for empathy and social relations. This reduces a huge source of stress, namely interpersonal relationships.

Kindness - an underestimated
intervention against stress

Sit down in a place where you can be undisturbed for a while. Start by being present, and following your breath for a few minutes. Reflect for a moment on the fact that all human beings are equal in a very fundamental way, namely that we all want to have satisfaction, joy and happiness, and that we all want to avoid dissatisfaction, pain and suffering. Let this basic fact sink in for a moment. Then ask yourself the following question: "What do I need from others in order to be satisfied, joyful and happy?" Think above all about what you need from others at work.

When thinking about this, your list is likely to include respect, appreciation and validation. It is important for you that others are present and pay attention when they talk to you. You appreciate when others are friendly and kind to you.

Once you have your list ready, think about the following questions, "What do others need from me to be satisfied, cheerful and happy?" You will probably realize that others need the same things from you that you require from them. In other words, it is important for others that you treat them with respect. It is important for others that you are kind and friendly towards them. It is important for others that you are present and pay attention to them when you speak with them. This applies to the cashier at the supermarket where you shop every day, it applies to your employees, your children and perhaps, unexpectedly, it applies to your manager.

Everyone wants to be treated with kindness.

Then, consider that research has shown that few phenomena contribute to stress as much as irritation and anger. Studies have even shown that our life is shortened if we are often angry.

Kindness is a neurological antidote against the state of mind of anger. If you train yourself to be present, open and friendly, you will counteract stress, not only in others, but perhaps most of all in yourself.

Consider how you can create a friendlier climate in your workplace to reduce stress in both your employees and yourself. Start with yourself and see what you can do to change your own attitude.

If you take the first step, it will affect others in your workplace and create positive spirals.

OAR - OBSERVE, ACCEPT, RELEASE

Stress reactions elicit habitual thought patterns in the form of negative thoughts that evoke feelings of discomfort and stress.

However, these thoughts are only one way to interpret events and ideas about yourself and others. They are not truths. Learn to recognize your automatic negative thoughts and try to find other intentional, balanced and realistic interpretations. These interpretations will in turn elicit other kinds of emotions.

Is it difficult? Then, try to imagine a friend in the same situation. What would you say to your friend? Probably the same can be applied to your situation.

Use the abbreviation OAR, that we have adapted from the mindfulness instructor Johan Bergstad, to remind yourself:

- **O:** observe when automatic thoughts arise.
- **A:** accept that they exist.
- **R:** release them.

You can use an internal picture as a means to let go of automatic thoughts. Put them on a bus, or see them as temporary guests at a cocktail party— say hello, exchange a few words and then say goodbye.

Be where you are

Do you want to be at home when you are at work or at work when you are home? If you want to be with the people or the life you have around you, don't open work emails at home, if you aren't prepared to do something about them. To think about problems at work in the evening (which you probably can't do anything about) doesn't make you a good parent, partner or friend. It probably raises the stress level when you should be unwinding.

Slow down

Start by deliberately walking slowly and try to use your senses. Breathe with your stomach, smell, feel, hear and observe your surroundings carefully. When you are stressed, you need to calm your system. Deliberately slowing down the tempo in the body helps this process. Therefore, you can also put down your cutlery after each well-chewed bite, try to brush your teeth very slowly and go slowly and attentively to a meeting at work.

You don't have control

Realize that you do not control the future, only this moment here and now. If there is a solution to a problem, it is needless to worry about it. If there is no solution to a problem, it is pointless to worry.

Prioritize

Make a list of things you want to do. Write the most important at the top. To focus consciously on one prioritized thing at a time counteracts stress.

Fake it 'til you make it

What usually makes you happy? What usually makes you laugh? Stress is a spoilsport and rarely initiates humor in life. Therefore, you need willpower to find it and get it into your life. Laughter and humor counteract stress.

Leave the computer

...phone and work outside your bedroom or at least your bed. To think of work when you go to sleep usually results in a bad night's sleep, which impairs your ability to manage external demands.

Clarify your job

Vague, undefined job descriptions with unclear deadlines and an unclear division of responsibilities is a major source of stress.

To work efficiently and stress free, find out exactly what is required of you.

Mind your own business 1

Trying to change someone else's behavior is often futile, so expend your energy on what *you* can influence and accept what *you* cannot change.

Be curious

Re-organizations are unavoidable because change is an on-going and inescapable occurrence. If you are afraid of new IT solutions or practices, see if they can instead awaken curiosity in you. To keep up, ask questions and try to learn new things. Keeping an open mind usually lessens internal stress.

Mind your own business 2

To compare yourself to others, especially people "better" than us, creates feelings of inadequacy and stress. Stop comparing yourself to others. Focus on what you have in your life. If you can't help but compare yourself to others, change your focus and compare yourself to those who really have a difficult life.

Find your niche in life

Do you know the stress of being in the wrong job in your professional life? Read about values in chapter 6 and find out what is meaningful in your life and in your work. Working in accordance with one's values counteracts stress.

Share yourself with others

Listen to others, show your appreciation, and say why you think someone is doing something well. Giving and receiving genuine confirmation reduces stress. People need to hear that what they are doing is meaningful and appreciated.

Learning to *observe* your thoughts, instead of *identifying* with them can *change* everything.

CHAPTER 4

WHAT IS MINDFULNESS?

DEFINITIONS AND BASIC EXERCISES

Your focus determines your reality.
Qui-Gon Jinn, Star Wars

Using examples from some work-related situations, we have discussed how increased internal and external demands can cause a stressed mind and inefficient behavior, in the form of multitasking. We have also described how we can learn to respond to the same situations in a focused and deliberate manner using mindfulness training.

Now, we will find out what the concept of mindfulness really means in concrete terms. This is our definition:

"Mindfulness is being attentive to and aware of what is happening right now in this moment, both internally and externally. That is all."

To explain the meaning of our definition, we want to flesh out the two concepts that are central to mindfulness and which depend on each other. They are directed and open attention, which we encountered in Chapter 2.

Directed attention is sometimes called focus or focused attention, and it is the ability to remain focused and concentrated on or absorbed by any part of an experience.

Open attention is sometimes called awareness, and it is the ability to be conscious of what we are experiencing—both what is going on within us (including bodily sensations, thoughts and feelings) and what is happening in our surroundings.

If directed attention is narrow and focused (preferably, as sharp as a laser beam), open attention is wide and more of a panoramic view.

Imagine your consciousness as a scene where different actors emerge. The cast comprises sensory input such as sound, sight and hearing, thoughts and memories—in short, all kinds of experiences that you can have. With directed attention, you can "zoom in" to a specific actor on this stage. With open attention, you can zoom out instead, and survey the whole scene—everything that is going on—both inside and outside—with an intense awareness. This is the opposite of daydreaming or being on mental "autopilot." Depending on the situation, you need to be able to switch between these two abilities—to zoom in and zoom out—as well as know the best place to zoom in.

This attention control is the basis of an ability that psychologists call metacognition, which is about being aware of how we think, feel and react. Metacognition is, in turn, the foundation for the optimal self-regulation of our behavior. When you are aware of your cognitive processes, then you are able to influence what you do, say and think in an optimal way. Mindfulness—the ability of focused and open attention—affects everything in your life and represents a kind of "basic conditioning" for your mind.

Other definitions of mindfulness usually include aspects of both directed and open attention, possibly with more weight given to open attention as the ability to develop an open, tolerant and observing attitude, highlighting one's personal experience. Directed attention and focus training has not previously been prevalent in mindfulness literature, but is found increasingly in research nowadays because of its fundamental function.

WHAT IS MINDFULNESS TRAINING?

Our definition of mindfulness training is: to train directed and open attention.

Neuroscientists have discovered that these two abilities, directed and open attention, are fundamentally important to determine how well our brains function (and, therefore, how well we function). They form the basis of all types of mental efficiency. They also form the basis of psychological well-being, which is perhaps a little more surprising. Brain researchers have discovered that these two abilities can be trained to a very high level, which is even more exciting.

Throughout this book, we describe how important these skills are in determining how we perform and how we feel. However, before we explore these concepts on a deeper level, let's take a few moments to reflect on how they affect our work.

What is your most important professional tool?

No, it's not your computer—at least not the one you have on your desk.

We would like to suggest that no matter whether you work as a nurse, lawyer, astrophysicist, politician, nanny or carpenter, the answer to the question is between your ears. Your brain, which is by far the most advanced thing in the known universe, has about 100 billion brain cells (neurons), each connected to thousands of others. Without this amazing device, you wouldn't last for a minute on the job.

The brain is your most important tool, which is obvious to some extent. Most of us have spent at least 15 years of our lives on education, which is intended to fill our brains with the information we need to perform our jobs.

The problem is that our Western culture tends to put too much emphasis on the abilities that involve retrieving and processing information. Of course, the information you have stored in your brain is likely to be critical to your job in one way or another, but the core capabilities of directed and open attention seem to have been overlooked to a large extent.

How useful is the *information* in your brain if you:

- Sit in an open-plan office and your attention is constantly "hijacked" by the noise around you, so you are not able to complete the report you are writing?
- See an elderly patient during a home visit and demonstrate a lack of attentiveness and empathy because your brain is busy planning the next visit, or thinking about what happened yesterday?
- Check your email every five minutes, which is something that you do unconsciously because the emails tend to trigger your anxiety or irritation?
- Are not able to be aware and present when questioning someone, thereby allowing subtle nuances to pass you by?

In the CBMT program, which is the basis for most of the exercises in this book, we usually present the two aspects of attention in a matrix. The matrix has two axes. One is directed attention, which goes from "distracted" to "focused." The other is open attention, which goes from "autopilot" to "aware."

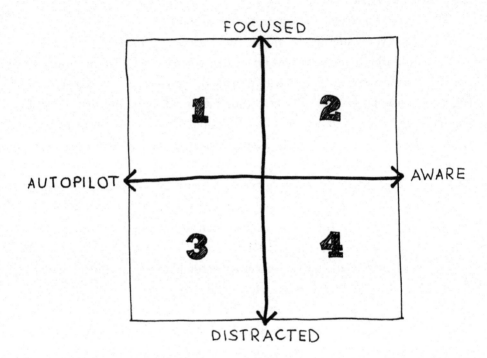

In this way, we get four quadrants. Now, imagine a situation at work where everything worked really well: a situation where you felt enthusiasm and interest, had lots of fun, and you were very efficient and productive as well. Which of the quadrants were you in?

It was in quadrant two, wasn't it?

This is what mindfulness training is all about—counteracting fragmented attention and developing a laser-sharp focus, as well as counteracting the brain's autopilot by developing a high level of awareness and presence.

The experience of mindfulness training in the workplace shows that it is usually important to begin by training directed attention or focus. This lays the foundation for training awareness.

In *The Attention Economy,* Thomas H. Davenport and John C. Beck describe how directed attention (which they call *"directed human attention"*) is by far the most valuable asset that companies have today. Directed attention has become hard currency. The reason is that companies have so much access to information, processes, support, knowledge and personnel, that the ability of people to control and direct their attention has become the bottleneck. What does it matter if we have the world's best IT systems with access to endless amounts of information if we lack the ability to recognize and make conscious choices and priorities?

When they wrote the book in 2001, Davenport and Beck were not aware that this ability can be trained. They had just identified how extremely important this was in order to create successful businesses.

William James, the founder of modern psychology, was aware of the value of being able to control one's attention quite early in the history of psychology. In his masterpiece, *The Principles of Psychology,* which he wrote in 1890, he said, "The faculty of voluntarily bringing back a wandering attention, over and over again, is the very root of judgment, character, and will. No one is compos sui if he have it not. An education which should improve this faculty would be the education par excellence." Unfortunately, he then goes on to conclude that it is "easier to define this ideal than to give practical directions for bringing it about." Only just over one hundred years after William James wrote his classic work, modern psychology has returned to the value of training the ability of directed attention. Imagine if James had had access to a brain scanner and had been able to see what scientists can today, that the training not only occurs, but also makes visible imprints in the brain!

Even though we now know that it is possible to practice directed attention, it doesn't mean that it is easy. Let us examine how attention actually works.

In *Strangers to Ourselves,* psychology professor Timothy D. Wilson explains that our brain is bombarded by 11 million bits of information every second.

At the same time, we only have the ability to be aware of 40 of these bits of information at any given moment. To illustrate how this works, think about when you put on your socks this morning. In that moment, you might have been aware of how your feet reacted to the light pressure of the sock, what the fabric felt like, or the warmth as you put on the socks.

If you focus on your feet now, can you feel your socks? You felt them this morning and you can feel them now. However, for the rest of the day, your feet have probably been walking around without your conscious awareness, while the sensory nerves in the feet dutifully continue to send information to your brain all day long. This has been part of the 11 million pieces of information that your brain receives every second, but you have not been aware of these sensations, because you have not directed your attention to them.

Attention can be described as a spotlight that illuminates a small part of our experience, which allows us to become aware of one particular thing (like our feet). The problem is that the spotlight is not particularly strong, and can only light up a very small area. It also constantly moves here and there, and it is difficult to keep it steady in one place. Imagine that you are trying to examine the wallpaper in a dark room with a torch. The cone of light is small and your hand is shaking a little, so that you can't keep the lamp still. It's quite difficult to see both the details and the overall pattern of the wallpaper.

Now, do a simple experiment. Direct your attention back to your feet and the sensation of your socks. Be as intensely aware of the details of sensory impressions as possible. Hold your attention on these sensations as long as you can, and don't think about anything else. Don't pay attention to any other sensory impressions. Try it now!

How long did you manage to keep your attention on your feet? If you are like most people, you held out for 3-4 seconds before your thoughts wandered off somewhere else. This is normal and nothing to worry about. At the same time, you can conclude that you don't have the world's best spotlight. The good news is that it can be improved. Studies on people who have been practicing mindfulness for a long time show that they can keep their attention on one point for several minutes.

However, as we have seen earlier, focusing on a single aspect of the experience is, of course, not an ability that is desirable in all situations. Often, we need a broader attention that makes us aware of the ever-changing flow of impressions that our brain is constantly processing.

Therefore you need to switch between these two types of attention: directed and open. This is what you do during mindfulness training—you take control of your focus, by utilizing directed attention, without letting yourself be distracted by disturbing impulses, and at the same time you are aware of everything going on within you and around you.

We end this chapter with two exercises to train focused and open attention, taken from the CBMT program.

ABCD - STRENGTHENING YOUR FOCUS

This is a basic mindfulness exercise to train directed attention. If you regularly do the ABCD exercise for ten minutes every day, you will experience a greater ability to be present with all the challenges you face during your working day. You will also increase your ability to let go of extraneous thoughts and distractions. An increased capacity for empathy is another more unexpected result. You will be able to maintain your attention on your colleagues, friends and family, without your mind wandering off.

Although this exercise is simple, the greatest challenge is to actually do it. Try to find a time each day when you can set aside ten minutes for the ABCD exercise—maybe in the morning, at lunch-time or in the evening. Find a time that works for you. The key here is regularity, because it facilitates the establishment of a new habit. Also, try to find a place where you can be relatively undisturbed, especially in the beginning. Once you have practiced for a while and are further down the track, it may be possible for you to do mindfulness training, for example, on the bus. In the beginning, however, there is a very high risk of distractions in such an environment.

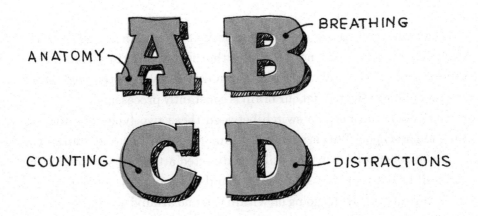

ABCD stands for:

A: Anatomy

The position of your body is not as crucial in mindfulness training, as it is an exercise for the brain. At the same time, it is helpful if you are sitting as comfortably as possible, so that your posture does not become a distraction. The following simple tips will also help you achieve the best possible conditions for your training:

- Sit on a chair with both feet on the ground. Be careful to sit in a balanced position without leaning forwards, backwards or sideways. It may be helpful to sit on the front edge of the seat.
- Sit with your back straight, but relaxed. Posture greatly influences your mental state. Sit upright with a posture that embodies alertness, attention and poise.
- Relax the whole body as much as possible, especially in the neck, shoulders and arms, which can be tense. Become aware of tensions and try to let go of them. It might be helpful to roll your shoulders a few times.
- Close your eyes completely. If you become drowsy, you can open them slightly, so that a little light comes in and activates the nervous system. If you open your eyes, rest your unfocused gaze at a point on the floor in front of you.
- Breathe through your nose during both inhalation and exhalation.

B: Breathing

When you close your eyes you'll find that your attention tends to wander to the past and future, and all over the place. You are training to focus your attention and, therefore, you need a focal point for your attention. In principle, it can be any object. Your breath is suitable to anchor your attention for two reasons. Firstly, it stimulates the parts of the nervous system that decrease stress reactions and helps coordinate the mind and body. Secondly, breathing is always with you for as long as you live, and you can learn to use it in all situations.

The instructions for observing the breath are simple:

- Focus all of your attention on the experience of breathing in the area of your stomach. Pay attention to how your abdomen rises as you inhale, and falls as you exhale. Become aware of all the physical sensations in your stomach.
- An alternative is to observe the breath in your nostrils. Be completely mindful of the experience of air, as it flows in and out with each breath. Focus on the stomach or the nostrils, depending on which is easier for you.
- Observe the breath in a neutral manner. You don't need to try to breathe deeply and slowly, or manipulate and alter the breath. You don't need to get involved with it at all, just let the breath take care of itself while you simply observe it neutrally, in the same way as you would observe waves crashing against a beach. This neutral observation can be challenging, but it is a crucial aspect of the training.

C: Counting

When you are sitting quietly and observing your breathing, you are quite likely to experience thoughts and distractions. Counting the breath can help remain focused. You will discover that each inhalation imparts new energy to the brain and a clearer focus, but it may be harder to maintain your attention on the exhalation, therefore counting in the following way may be helpful:

- Inhale, then exhale, and at the end of the exhalation, count "one." On the next exhalation, count "two." Continue in this way up to ten. When you reach ten, count in the same way back down to one. Continue counting from one to ten and back, again and again.

- If you don't get further than three or seven, don't worry, that's normal. With a little practice, you will notice that it will begin to change.

- If you suddenly discover that you have reached 17, that means that the autopilot has been turned on and you haven't been paying attention. Start from one again. If you realize that you aren't counting any longer, start from one in the same way.

- You will notice that many thoughts creep in between the numbers. This is a sign that you are not fully aware of the breath. Sharpen your focus.

- Most people find counting very helpful, especially in the beginning. About 15 per cent of people experience it as a distraction instead. If you are one of them, ignore the counting and just focus on your breath. For some, counting helps at certain times, but not for others. Let go of it, if it isn't helping.

D: Distractions

The last of the four instructions are the distractions. They are your challenge, but also your greatest teacher. Despite counting, you might find that you have become distracted occasionally (or, maybe the whole time). The distractions arise from your six senses: smell, taste, touch, hearing, sight and consciousness itself. As you are sitting quietly with your eyes closed, most of the senses will be disconnected, so the primary sources of the distractions are hearing and consciousness (in the form of thoughts, memories etc.).

No matter what the distraction is, the simple instruction is that when you discover that you have become distracted, follow these three steps: relax, release, return.

- *Relax:* A normal reaction when one becomes distracted is to become frustrated and tense up a little. This doesn't help at all, it is better to relax instead. Just notice that you have been distracted, and see the distraction as a good friend who reminds you that your attention has wandered off.

- *Release:* Let go of the distraction with the gratitude that it showed you that you went off track.
- *Return:* Return to your breathing with renewed attention and focus.

EXERCISE IN OPEN ATTENTION

As we have already mentioned, the training in directed attention is closely connected to the training in open attention. Training in focus calibrates and sharpens your "mental microscope"—you strengthen your ability to focus on whatever you wish. When training open attention, you widen your inner microscope to include everything that is going on. The focus is no longer the breath, but the distractions instead.

Your task is to observe your thoughts, feelings and sensations quite neutrally, like a scientist in your own mental laboratory. In this way, you will get a better understanding of your own thoughts and habitual patterns. When you have reached this point, you can start to focus your attention in such a way that you strengthen the thoughts and habits that are beneficial and alter or remove those that are not.

First, follow the instructions in directed attention using the ABCD model above. Then, after a few minutes, take the exercise in a different direction:

- In the same way as the focus training exercise, start by sitting comfortably, which we described in "Anatomy" above.
- Focus your full attention on the breath for one or two minutes, just as in focus training. Let the mind become steady and quiet. Count your breaths if this is helpful. Let go of distractions.
- Then, begin your training in open attention. Let go of the focus on the breath and widen your attention to include everything that is going on in your consciousness. When the first distraction makes itself known (a sound, a thought, a physical sensation or something else), move your full attention to it and use it as an anchor for your attention.
- Observe the distraction neutrally, just as you did previously with the breath, without following any trains of thought, or pushing them away, or trying to manipulate or control your experience. Be neutral, as if you were observing waves crashing on a beach.

- Note when a distraction occurs, when it is still present and when it has disappeared or changed. When a distraction ceases, be open to approach the next one in the same way. If the distraction is changing, just follow the transformation neutrally.
- If at any time you feel that everything is just pouring in and making a big mess—that distractions are piling up and making everything muddy—move your attention back to your breath to stabilize again. After a few moments, when your attention is more stable, let go of the breath and open your attention again. You can always return to the stable and reliable anchor of the breath.
- If you find that it is difficult to observe the distraction neutrally and you notice that you have become involved with it, then give it a mental "label." For example, if the idea of a shopping list pops up and you can't let it go, label the idea as "shopping list." Putting labels on distractions in this way is a great help to "neutralize" them.

The instructions are simple—they are not mysterious nor difficult to understand. The biggest challenge for most people is to maintain their position as a neutral observer when the distractions are interesting. You can't overestimate the mental strength and freedom that you develop by mastering this technique. Learning to observe your thoughts, instead of identifying with them, can change everything.

One way to *describe the effects* of mindfulness is that it enables you to create a space that allows you to make informed choices.

CHAPTER 5

WHY ARE YOU WORKING?

ABOUT THE IT MANAGER WHO REALLY BECAME A LEADER, THE ARTIST WHO FOUND JOY IN A GLUE GUN AND HOW TO CREATE SUSTAINABILITY FOR YOURSELF AND YOUR ORGANIZATION

MADISON, 53, WAS A SENIOR MANAGER AT A LARGE IT COMPANY. She thrived on the job, performed extremely well and directed most of her energy towards making perfect quarterly reports. She was primarily motivated by the continual applause she received from management. Her employees were used to seeing her fixed smile as she quickly walked past in the corridor, looking straight ahead. In her private life, Madison rarely missed her son's football training, family dinner parties or booking the summer holiday in time.

When Madison began practicing mindfulness, it was because she wanted to sharpen her mental skills and perform even better. The training gave her the results she had hoped for quite quickly. She became considerably less stressed, had a sharper focus and experienced an increased internal stability.

However, the greatest and most unexpected result of her mindfulness training was the realization that she was living her life "in her head." Madison became aware of how her sharp intellect dominated her existence, and that everything in her life revolved around planning, structuring, problem solving and abstract thinking.

"I thought I knew what I wanted in life, and what was important for me, but when I started practicing mindfulness, I made a deeper connection with myself. It may sound irrational, but for the first time in my life, I discovered my "gut feeling." It was as if I had lived life on the surface and for the first time I came into contact with all of me. It was as though everything was beginning to make sense."

Getting into contact with her emotions also meant that Madison became aware of her values. However, what many people may be scared of when they really get in contact with their feelings, didn't happen. Madison didn't change her whole life externally to become a volunteer in Tanzania, so she could feel that she was making a difference. Instead, she found deeper meaning in the work she already had.

"The most transformative awareness was that I suddenly understood why it was important for me to be the boss. It was not about career, recognition or even exciting challenges. It was that I actually had the opportunity to make a big difference in people's lives—in my employees' lives. The insight that I could be the manager, not for my own sake, but for others, was almost a shock to me.

On a practical level, this realization meant that Madison began to prioritize differently. She decreased the time she spent on administration and the detailed examination of strategies, and instead began to devote more time and attention to really understand her colleagues, listen to them and encourage them. On the basis of this awareness, she also began to facilitate change in the lives of her employees in a practical way.

The unity that Madison felt within herself when she let out her emotions along with her intellect, was also something she experienced in relation to her colleagues, resulting in a greater coherence between her newfound appreciation and how she dealt with everyday situations.

"When I saw and understood why I reacted as I did in each situation in my life, then I could start changing. One can say that mindfulness has given me both a direction and an ability to take each step in that direction."

As we have mentioned, mindfulness has two dimensions: attention and awareness. This chapter deals primarily with the second aspect—awareness.

Attention is about the ability to be present; awareness refers to the way we pay attention and what we place our attention on. Applied to the world of work, it can be said that this aspect of mindfulness is about increasing our awareness of why we work, but also about how we work.

If you feel frustrated by your work situation and are stuck in a thought loop about whether you should change jobs or not, we would like to encourage you to change focus for a while and explore these particular issues.

Once you have done that, you will most likely know what to do, and be able to identify your next step in your working life and your life in general.

In Google's mindfulness training program *"Search Inside Yourself,"* they talk about developing high-resolution awareness. It draws a parallel between our human consciousness and the image of a modern high-resolution TV (rather than an old TV with low resolution). What this means is that mindfulness training provides a more distinct and clear awareness of how we behave and the consequences of this behavior, both for ourselves and for others. Behavior, in this instance, includes the whole spectrum of thoughts, actions, emotions, habits and values.

People who have been practicing mindfulness often describe similar results to Madison. In the beginning, they experience immediate effects, such as less stress, better quality sleep and increased focus. Then, as the training continues, they begin to report a deeper change—a better understanding of themselves and others. They often re-evaluate what is truly important in life. For many, this leads to more fulfilling and meaningful work, where they find their way back to the qualities they may have lost along the way, like enthusiasm, joy and commitment.

What does it mean to train "awareness"?

Our senses are the instruments through which we perceive ourselves and the world around us. When you train mindfulness, you strengthen and refine your contact with this instrument. The more you develop the ability to experience the five senses (sight, sound, touch, smell and taste), the more awareness you will experience. The world is then perceived in "high resolution," i.e. more finely tuned.

In turn, this awareness has two aspects. You will become more aware of life as a whole—"the big picture"—which is linked to your values. This helps you answer questions such as: what is important to me in my life? Why am I doing the work that I do? What do I want to achieve and why? What do I want to contribute? What is rewarding, stimulating and interesting for me?

In the second aspect, you become more aware of what is happening in each moment. By seeing clearly how your own thoughts, feelings and habitual patterns express themselves, you increase your ability to make wise decisions in the present moment—a decision that is in line with "the big picture."

Through mindfulness training, you can view both aspects simultaneously: the wider perspective revealing the long-term impact of your direct action in each moment.

An employment agency did a study in 2012 to investigate the job satisfaction of their employees. The results were quite disappointing, as well as remarkable. Only 19 per cent responded that they were satisfied with their work. Another 16 per cent were "partially satisfied." The rest—nearly two thirds—said that they didn't enjoy their work.

The fact that so many of us are not satisfied with about half of our lives, is something that has astonished the Dalai Lama, among others. In an interview when responding to the question about what surprised him most about mankind, he said something to the effect of, "People sacrifice their health to make money, and then spend money to regain their health. They are so worried about the future that they are not enjoying the present. The result is that they don't live in the present or in the future. They live as if they will never die, and when they die, it is as though they never really lived."

How did this happen? Why is the part of life that involves work not a source of enthusiasm, meaning and development for so many people? Does it need to be like this?

THE JOY OF A GLUE GUN

Linda Nordfors is an artist and part of the minority that enjoys work very much.

In 2001 she founded Sweden's first art agency with the mission statement to create art in order to build brands. In her own journey to find a way to earn a living from what she loves to do, she has conceptualized what she provocatively calls "The art of selling your heart." Using that as a starting point, she conducts courses and lectures in sales for those who want to earn a living from what they are passionate about.

When Linda was asked why she thinks so many of us don't choose a job that we enjoy, she says that there is a widespread idea that real work is something that is difficult and tedious. Work is often seen as suffering, and a salary is seen as compensation for this suffering. Too many people live with the unspoken notion that if something is meaningful and important to them, they can't charge for or receive payment for doing it. It makes them feel guilty.

"The unfortunate consequence of not questioning their own view of real work, is that they unconsciously seek out something that they don't really like. However, it doesn't need to be like that", says Linda.

"If we become conscious of what is actually important to us in life, then we are laying the foundation to be able to turn our attention to doing what feels meaningful, riveting and rewarding for us, even at work."

In her lectures and courses, Linda usually talks about her own process, which started with a glue gun.

"It's a trivial example and that's why it works so well. Finding what we want to do in life doesn't necessarily mean something really huge. It can begin with something that is pure joy. We just want to do something, and sometimes we don't even know why. The challenge we face, whether we are employees or contractors, is to explain how what we want to do creates value for others—employers, customers or our world. Personally, I think it's great fun to work with a glue gun, and I'm also very good at it. Why would my desire to glue things together make what I glue less valuable? The opposite is actually true. The more passion, the greater the chance that the result is outstanding."

Using joy in her glue-gun as a starting point, Linda began to consider how she could create art out of that. The idea was to combine objects that normally don't belong together.

The idea became a reality when Linda approached a company that manufactured panty liners, with the proposal of using them to make dresses. Since then, Linda has created a variety of spectacular dresses that have become a big PR success.

"My part of the project was about the pure joy of creation. At the same time, it contained an exciting message where the intimate became external, the shameful was flaunted, and the secret was made visible. Just doing this was meaningful for me, which increased when I noticed how the artworks influenced other people's pride in their work. An employee of the company exclaimed, 'Of course, this is beautiful.' She had been on the job for 15 years and hadn't seen the beauty in what she held in her hands!"

The pure joy of creation has not always been self-evident for Linda. Previously, she was trapped in the external notions of what work should represent. In her case, money was not the driving force; however, it was necessary for each project to clearly contribute to improving the world. She discovered quite soon that most of this led to a guilty conscience.

"It wasn't enough to have an intellectual understanding that 'what I do is good for so and so' somewhere a long way down the chain of events. The challenge is to ask myself, 'What do I like to do?' and listen to the answer. It is more important than we might like to admit, even to ourselves. However, many people are downright scared to look inwardly. I think the fear stems from some sort of projection about not being good enough and a belief that what you feel is not relevant, valid, or important. At the same time, people are also afraid that they will find something that is so powerful that it will decimate their entire existence. This is the paradox as I see it—someone might be longing for revolutionary change, but they are also afraid of it. It is a fear of lifting the lid, but there is something meaningful under the lid, or that's where their purpose will be found. Purpose is like love, it is present all the time, but the experience of it comes and goes."

This "mishmash"—as Linda calls it—the fear of one's own strength and the cultural misconception that paid work can't also be meaningful is the reason why many people choose not to look inward, according to Linda. "Many feel that if they receive a salary, then they're indebted to their employers and have no right to claim meaningfulness. Money can really create a sense of guilt."

However, Linda says that there's no reason for guilt or any discrepancy between money and meaningfulness—on the contrary, especially not from an employer's perspective.

"The best chance for an employer to develop company values is to create loyalty and a team spirit. If you can create purpose and a sense of context, you get dedicated and loyal employees. We must let money fulfill its function, i.e. as a practical means of bartering. I am helping with something that is important to my clients, and when I contribute my skills, I receive money because the client can't offer me anything I need. It is an interaction that doesn't need to be loaded with guilt, greed or a constant desire for more."

In her courses, Linda encourages participants to find out what they want to get involved with. It is an awareness process, which is exciting, fun, inspiring and meaningful. It's not a selfish process because it benefits everyone.

"The more we are in our element, the more value we can contribute. It's not that we think it's child's play all the time—the meaningful can often be difficult and challenging as well, but these challenges can be met if we are doing something that we feel is worthy of our attention. We have so much more potential to contribute than we realize."

Things are changing, and it's easy to cling to the past. Linda's challenge is that we remain curious and open-minded about ourselves.

"Open up! People who are closed off don't know when they are in their element. We can only know when we are mindful and when we are aware."

SWEDEN – THE LAND OF MODERATION

To further understand the challenges for Swedes in finding meaning at work, we can take a global viewpoint. Every five years, a global cultural map is published—the World Values Map—which charts human values. This explains the 70 per cent difference in people's behavior based on two valuation methods:

1. Self-realization versus survival values.
2. Traditional versus rational and secular values.

In countries with a strong survival assessment, people focus on having a roof over their heads, finding food each day and avoiding injury. When these needs are met, the focus is naturally more on self-realization.

The second method is about tradition-bound values with strong religious elements and/or family values versus secular and rational values, in which you, as an individual, can choose your own direction.

It turns out that Sweden—the land of moderation—is the most extreme land in both of these two types of measurements. We are the highest in self-realization and the second highest in the rational/secular category. Each time the survey has been done, the distance from other countries on the World Values Map has increased. This is true, especially among younger people.

Stefan Ekwall is a consultant at an organization with a similar purpose to that of Linda, which is to help managers and employees live and work authentically and sustainably and be "self-determined." He has contemplated the extreme values of Swedes based on the cultural map and believes that this attitude is nearing the end of the road. He suggests that they can't do any further self-realization on an individual, secular and material level and, therefore, they need to search for other values in common that are durable. He sees this desire particularly in young people, who generally have higher expectations that work not only provides money, but is also meaningful. He explains:

"People complain a lot that generation Y (born in the 80s and 90s) is spoiled, but there is also a strength in having grown up in a very safe community with thousands of options, because then they start asking lots of questions. There is a growing requirement that they want to be connected to a purpose, which provides motivation and energy. Fortunately, companies are beginning to understand this and are willing to do something about it. Many business leaders see it as a success factor to be a values-driven company, but few know how to do this."

As we mentioned earlier, values consist in being conscious of both the "big picture" and an awareness of how one behaves in relation to the big picture. Sustainability occurs when both of these agree with one another.

Stefan says that to in order to be sustainable, a person needs to develop authenticity, i.e. remain the same person in all circumstances and not differentiate between values at work and values at home. This is important, not only for your own sense of purpose, but also on a group level.

"If you are authentic, you can't, for example, recycle at home and then go to work and make a decision that says the opposite—you wouldn't be living according to your principles."

Stefan believes that work satisfaction suffers because we often leave not only our values, but also our feelings at home, when we go to work and, unfortunately, this behavior is reinforced by the rational work culture in the West.

"Unfortunately, companies usually formulate values that are on a mental, not an emotional level. It is standard to inform employees about the way we work and what the organization stands for. This is something that employees may be able to understand, but if they can't connect emotionally to the values, they will feel no real commitment. Then, there is an imminent risk that they also won't choose to act in line with the company's direction and values."

Stefan's solution to counteract futility and dissatisfaction on the job is the same as for Madison and Linda—by getting in contact with one's emotions and improving the awareness of what we have in common. In his own words, "Find your own driving force and try to understand and support each other emotionally, not just intellectually." This reinforces the feeling of connection and meaning."

"In a practical way, we can train our compassion in every meeting with colleagues. This can also be done by introducing a "check-in-time" at the beginning of group meetings, where participants can say a few words about what they think is important right now. Those who wish to may begin. Keep it short and make it as practical as possible. There is always a social code of relating and the rule of thumb is: stretch your comfort zone, but don't over-do it! This strengthens relationships, increasing the presence of each and everyone, and helps people express their opinions later in the meeting.

Stefan's experience is that these introductory exercises provide more perspectives and, therefore, increase the ability to solve problems. This exercise has also proved to lower participant blood pressure levels!

Another suggestion is to encourage employees to actively support prevailing corporate values.

"In our courses, employees reflect on how important the values of the organization are for them personally, as well as assessing how they and the company are working in accordance with them. Then you become involved, even if someone else has developed values. I would say that, in 99 cases out of 100, you can find your own meaning in the existing values of the organization—if there is room for self-reflection and insight."

Some of those who have been taking the values-based mindfulness courses are students at the Stockholm School of Economics. Since 2012, there has been an optional course that Stefan Ekwall has been involved in developing. He remembers that, before the course started, the director expressed the fear that people would drop out of education if they came into contact with what they really think is important. As this book is being written, this fear has not yet materialized.

"The fact is that when you discover what is truly important for you personally, you realize you have a tool that enables you to be proactive in your environment. You may be thinking, "Soon I'll be working, and then I'll know what my personal values are, and I'll be able to use the tools I have learnt here to make a difference." Many people have made this conclusion, which has strengthened their self-determination."

Stefan believes that Sweden has a unique position to be a pioneer as a value-driven country.

"Most countries are moving in our direction—towards rational values and self-fulfillment—but now we're moving beyond self-fulfillment. By taking advantage of the need for meaning and belonging that is beginning to emerge here, we can show the way for other countries—in how to build strong organizations with steadfast co-workers, and how all of us can build a sustainable world."

come up with. Then ask yourself, "What is the meaning of life?" Other answers are likely to arise from that question.

We often have the tendency to separate work from the rest of our life. Working is something we do in order to do what we really want to do— later. However, if there is meaning in life, then there should be the same meaning in work. Work is a part of our lives, and for most of us, it is a very central, time-consuming and important part. If we want to find meaning in our work, then we need to think about the meaning of life in general.

BE HAPPY AND AVOID SUFFERING

Let's highlight some basic biological and psychological facts about people, which may help you to understand your motivations and perhaps make it easier for you to see the meaning of your (working) life.

We are biological organisms and we are driven by two very basic and primary driving forces. The first is a desire to experience pleasure, satisfaction, joy and happiness. The second is a desire to avoid discomfort, suffering and pain. These desires can ultimately be seen as a consequence of wanting to live and avoiding death.

This is neither good nor bad, that is just how it is. All living creatures want to live and avoid death. Everyone wants to be happy and avoid suffering. Happiness is expressed differently in different people (we will return to this), but generally we all aim for some kind of happiness, while we are doing our utmost to avoid pain and discomfort.

Given this, we would like to give the following as a possible answer to the question about the meaning of life: to be happy and avoid suffering and help others be happy and avoid suffering.

Suppose then that the division between meaning in work and meaning in the rest of life is unnecessary. The division is merely a mental construction that we are free to interpret. This means that our purpose could, in fact, also be the whole point of working. In other words: to be happy and avoid suffering and helping others be happy and avoid suffering.

We are aware that this assertion sounds deceptively simple, but obviously it is not so easy. Do you remember the statistics? Only 19 per cent of the people in that 2012 survey were satisfied with their jobs. The majority perceived their work as a source of dissatisfaction, pain and suffering.

Different kinds of happiness

There is a whole area of psychology that deals with the question of what makes people happy. Positive psychology was founded by Martin Seligman and Mihaly Csikszentmihalyi in the late 1990s as an alternative to a psychology that had been focused for over a hundred years only on different psychiatric diagnoses and how they can be cured.

Positive psychology aims to explore how to make life more meaningful and joyful, rather than just treat mental illness. The central themes are about helping people develop their strengths and virtues, as well as increasing the experiences of social interaction—at work and in private.

What we want to highlight here is that, in the research on positive psychology, there is usually a distinction between the two types of happiness: hedonic and eudaimonic. Hedonic happiness is about doing things that immediately result in a positive experience and state of mind. Simply put, hedonic happiness occurs when we experience pleasure. This means that if you are able to enjoy your work, you will also appreciate it more.

Meanwhile, it has been shown that for happiness to be stable and enduring, it also needs to be eudaimonic. This feeling is more about being part of a social context, to contribute to other people's well-being, as well as have a more wide-ranging and greater purpose for actions than instant gratification.

There is a study that presented some astonishing findings regarding genetics and hedonic versus eudaimonic happiness. It showed that people who were more hedonically oriented towards the immediate satisfaction of their needs (for example, consumption) had a genetic profile with relatively high levels of biological markers linked to higher levels of inflammation in the body, which in turn increase the risk of developing cancer, diabetes and cardiovascular diseases. Those who had a more eudaimonic focus in life had a different genetic profile, with a higher degree of antibody production and lower degree of pro-inflammatory gene expression.

Scientists aren't able to explain what causes this, but it appears that we are programmed at the genetic level for different social behaviors.

That is not to say that people are doomed to pre-determined patterns in life. Genetics are also affected by our behavior, which is something we can change through willpower—particularly with the help of mindfulness training, which has been shown to enhance feelings and behaviors related to eudaimonic happiness.

To clarify: There is nothing wrong with enjoyment—the more fun and enjoyment we can have on the job, the better. However, it seems to be important for our well-being that we are also motivated by long-term and higher purposes.

From short-term to long-term

Linked to the issue of hedonic and eudaimonic happiness is the understanding of the mechanisms behind how we manage short-term and long-term consequences. This is something that gets us into trouble in life because our actions are generally governed more by a short-term than a long-term perspective, which tends to make us more unhappy.

Take, for example, the meeting where you lashed out at your overbearing colleague with a cutting remark, and gave him/her a real dressing-down, which seemed so appropriate in the moment. Later, when you thought back on the situation, you may have felt uncomfortable. Is it possible that your behavior was rash, low and unjust? You probably reacted as you did, because it gave you two short-term rewards: by going on the attack, you avoided discomfort (irritation, frustration or fear) that the colleague aroused in you for some reason. Additionally, you probably got some instant gratification out of positive emotions—it may have felt good to get really angry and put someone in their place.

Afterwards you can possibly rationalize yelling, and convince yourself that you stood up for yourself, did not take any rubbish and that it's good to be honest and tell it like it is. However, if you investigate your behavior, you can see that you were controlled by an immediate desire to be free from the discomfort you experienced in the moment.

It can be useful to be clear about this. It's not necessarily wrong to put your foot down when you have been mistreated. The difference lies in being aware of the underlying purpose of your conduct. Instinctively scolding someone because there is discomfort in your body that you want to avoid is one thing. It is quite another to reflect on the long-term consequences, and come to the conclusion that a scolding would be most beneficial, both for yourself and the colleague. If you have the presence of mind to reflect on the long-term benefits for yourself and others, it is very seldom that you will decide to act harshly. You will usually find wiser and more constructive ways to achieve what you really want.

One of the major effects of practicing mindfulness is that you become more aware that you are often guided by short-term consequences of your behavior. This process is often unconscious and automatic. Something happens that you respond to immediately, without thinking.

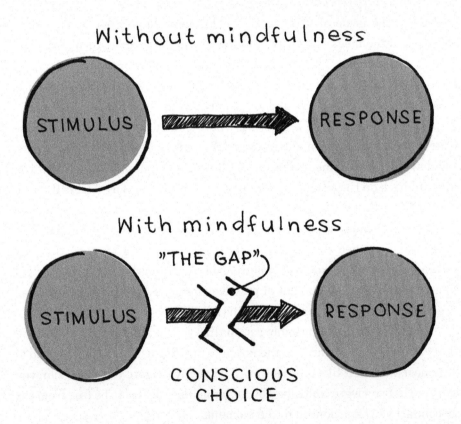

Psychologists call what happens a *stimulus*, and our behavior the *response* (see the diagram above).

One way to describe the effects of mindfulness is that you create a "gap" between the stimulus and the response. This is a space that allows you to make informed choices, which is the same as the "extra second" of which Jacob spoke in chapter 3. Mindfulness training gives you an extra moment of consideration, with more mental freedom. When you create this space for wise choices, you can ensure that your behavior is in harmony with your values and the broader perspective, instead of just reacting automatically to avoid discomfort or to gain a momentary short-term advantage.

In this way, the two aspects of mindfulness are linked together—you are aware of your values associated with the choices you make in each moment. Awareness, presence and attention thereby help you to make wise choices that contribute to both your own and other people's happiness and well-being.

Here is a series of examples of common conflict situations that may arise at work. In the first column, we describe some habitual, automatic behavior controlled by short-term consequences in the second column, and the long-term consequences in the third column. Under each example, we give suggestions on how to respond to the same situation using mindfulness, in a conscious way.

Example of a common job situation followed by automatic behavior	Short-term consequence of the automatic behavior	Long-term consequence of the automatic behavior
A colleague comes and asks for help from Steven, who immediately gets a lump in his stomach. He already has enough to do, but to say no feels uncomfortable. Steven is also flattered, so he agrees to help.	Steven avoids the discomfort of saying no to his colleague. In addition, he gets a positive feeling out of making the colleague happy when he says yes.	Steven takes on too much work, and becomes increasingly fragmented and stressed. In the end, he can't manage to do his work properly, because the load just keeps growing.

Possible alternative conscious behavior: Steven is aware of the discomfort that occurs in his body when he is asked for help. He realizes that it is a temporary, harmless and transient feeling. He is also aware that saying "yes" is unsustainable in the long-term. So, instead of immediately following the impulse to say "yes," Steven pauses and gives himself a few seconds to reflect before responding. During this time, he is making a conscious and sustainable decision, which in this case is to say no.

Example of a common job situation followed by automatic behavior	Short-term consequence of the automatic behavior	Long-term consequence of the automatic behavior
Tina blames her colleague, Paul, for losing an important customer contract. Paul feels unfairly singled out. Initially, he is sad and disappointed, but almost immediately that feeling turns into anger. His body tightens, his pulse increases, his face becomes red and Paul chastises Tina, calling her all sorts of names.	Yelling decreases tension in the body, and Paul's discomfort evaporates as he comes into contact with his sad feelings. As well as this, it feels good—almost pleasurable—to be able to scold Tina.	Tina feels attacked, and is hurt by the harsh words spoken by Paul. This has damaged the capacity for trust and co-operation between the two colleagues. The job satisfaction of both Paul and Tina decreases.

Possible alternative conscious behavior: Paul notices his sadness and then anger rising internally. He can also feel how his body is tightening and that his breathing is higher up in his chest. He breathes air into his abdomen, and notices how this action reduces the tension and anger. It also helps him to remember the customer contract and think about what has happened. Everything takes place within one or two seconds. He observes Tina's face and notices how disappointed she looks. This short observation, which he communicates to Tina, starts a discussion about what really happened and what they can do together to solve the problem.

Example of a common job situation followed by automatic behavior	Short-term consequence of the automatic behavior	Long-term consequence of the automatic behavior
Sally does "overtime" on a report till late at night.	Sally feels a sense of control that reduces the discomfort of handing in an unfinished report. She also has the rewarding feeling of being a good and productive employee.	The fact is that Sally rarely ever catches up. She never has enough time, for the simple reason that it isn't possible to be completely in control or attain perfection. Therefore, she lives with a constant feeling of inadequacy.

Possible alternative conscious behavior: Sally keeps track of what is really important and high priority in both her work and in life in general. She learns to cope with the uncertainty and the feeling of inadequacy without letting her behavior be controlled by this.

Example of a common job situation followed by automatic behavior	Short-term consequence of the automatic behavior	Long-term consequence of the automatic behavior
A colleague gets fired for what John perceives to be unjust reasons. John gets upset, but fails to take up the matter with HR.	By failing to take up the matter, John will not have the discomfort of risking being criticized and questioned.	Uneasy thoughts gnaw away at John, and his dissatisfaction with his employer continues. His situation remains unchanged. The director, who in fact would appreciate forthright feedback, notices that John seems unengaged and mentally distracted.

Possible alternative conscious behavior: John goes directly to HR and takes up "the problem" in a friendly, straightforward and constructive manner. He faces the discomfort without letting himself be hindered by it.

This provides the optimum conditions for constructive change. Additionally, a lot of energy is released that would otherwise fuel worry and irritation.

Example of a common job situation followed by automatic behavior	Short-term consequence of the automatic behavior	Long-term consequence of the automatic behavior
Murray is surfing the Web instead of planning an important meeting.	It's more fun to watch cats playing, than write an agenda.	The agenda isn't written, and the meeting is poorly prepared. Murray has divided his attention, which impairs his ability to focus and be present.

Possible alternative conscious behavior: Murray remembers the two rules for mental efficiency:

1. Focus on what you choose (in this case, planning the meeting) and remain on-task.
2. Consciously let go of distractions (the cats).

When Murray has written his agenda, he notices that there is also time to laugh at the cats, which he does with a clear conscience.

Compassion and mindfulness

An experimental study shows how people who have done eight weeks of mindfulness training were equally quick to help a person in difficulty as those who specifically meditated on compassion. Both groups were, in turn, five times as fast to the rescue as the people who had not meditated in any form.

The fact that the mindfulness group was as compassionate as the second group, is due to an increased capacity to take different perspectives, and a greater awareness that has been well-developed in mindfulness training, according to researchers.

TIPS

Time for conversation and reflection

Take time to consider what is truly important to you and examine how it can manifest itself in your workplace. Use conversation – dare to speak, listen and be open with your intentions and feelings, as both employee and manager. Many are afraid to be open, for fear of being ostracized or fired. The fact is that most people appreciate open people.

By starting to become open yourself, you lay the foundation for a more trusting work environment, which benefits you and everyone else, and also increases your overall problem-solving ability.

What is the point of doing things in a way that ends up taking longer, has a worse result and requires more effort?

CHAPTER 6

THE CONSULTANT WHO SOUGHT HAPPINESS

ABOUT PRODUCTIVITY – A WAY TO RELAX

*When my mind is in overdrive, I feel that it isn't
functioning optimally and then I release the tension.
It's like stepping on the clutch while driving – you don't
accelerate or brake. My perspective returns and my
thinking goes from black and white to color. My whole job
is to give advice, and my mind is my tool of trade,
so it needs to be alert.*
Carl, management consultant

Carl, 31, studied Industrial Management at Linköping University of Technology before he got a job at an international management consulting firm—a company known for attracting ambitious, career-minded and high-performing individuals. Carl was one of them. He stayed on for a year, and then applied to work at a large Swedish company, still as a consultant. At both companies, he invested long hours and complete dedication to contribute to high productivity. However, at the international firm, this effort resulted in exhaustion, and after a while, also declining productivity. Here is Carl's story of what happened, explaining why he started mindfulness training, and how he raised his productivity through relaxation:

"AT THE INTERNATIONAL COMPANY, people were working around 60 hours a week—ranging between 50 and 80 hours. It was often more than that, when travelling. As a management consultant, you are constantly working against a deadline. Usually, after three months, you have to complete what your client has requested. Every week there is a reconciliation with your partner or project manager, and meetings that need to be prepared and evaluated. You are constantly on the run. It's like more education after having finished university, and after two and a half or three years, many leave. It often leads to a better job. These companies also have the policy of putting the "customer first," which puts a lot of pressure on their employees. There were countermeasures in place. From time to time, they plotted graphs measuring two items. One was the happiness of the team, based on a survey every week, where they responded to various questions about how well the team was doing. The other factor was how many hours you worked. If you saw project after project were people weren't happy and worked long ours, you didn't want to work with that project manager again. It was a good idea, and it worked to a degree, partly because there were discussions about why things turned out the way they did. However, it's fairly difficult to get away from the overall set-up. There are many experts, but they can only be used through a consultant, such as myself. Therefore, the consultant becomes the eye of the needle that all things must go through. The more hours of thought and effort the consultant puts in, the more the customer gets out of the company. On average, I worked 65 hours a week.

Now I have the same consultant role where I am today, but I have a smaller group, with 30 people instead of 300, and we are only working internally. We aren't driven by results or bonuses in the same way as at the previous company. It isn't based as much on financial success.

In an environment such as in the last company, it is harder to be mindful. You had to be better at mindfulness in order to manage the workload, because of the fast pace. It would have been easier to be mindful if I raked leaves in a cemetery. In my role, it is more difficult, because it is necessary to use my mind in a demanding way, especially if there is more stress. This results in tunnel vision, which makes it even harder. It might have been possible to continue working at my old job with my health intact, but it would have been very challenging.

I had a couple of projects at the international company that required fairly long hours. One was in Germany where I sometimes worked until 1 or

2 or even 3 a.m., and then I was up at 7 a.m. the next morning. There were quite a few weekends. The mind is our tool, but it doesn't work as well with sleep deprivation and stress. All of this was counterproductive, but I didn't notice it then. I felt very pressured, but I thought, this is the way it is.

My mind didn't get to rest and I never got enough sleep. On a few occasions, I woke up at 7 a.m. on a Sunday, got dressed, and thought I was late for a meeting, before I realized it was Sunday.

This should have been a warning sign, but I bought it. The positive aspect is that the whole time, it feels like you are important. You work in a team and you are constantly challenged. You are well paid and you're working with important issues. You go around in a suit, which is a trigger for the ego. I still have a role where I go around in a suit and work with important issues, but now I have a completely different understanding of how the mind works.

The change occurred after working like that for six months, when I was on holiday over the summer. It was a time for much contemplation and questioning. When I did my internship, I had very good mentors and colleagues, but when I started as a consultant, I felt that it was no longer fun. It made me wonder if I had other options. When you have started this type of reflection, things begin to happen. I found a group that I liked, which I am in now, and it was a fairly easy step for me to change jobs. At the same time, it was a smaller step than what I experienced when I began to dedicate myself to things related to mindfulness.

My father was ill the whole of last year, and he was diagnosed with cancer last spring. It puts things in perspective and makes you start thinking. I'm good at problem solving. When you find a solution to a problem, you are on the path to your goal. What is the ultimate goal in life? I began to think about this question. I started looking at words like "happiness." Did it possibly relate to what is important in my life? I started doing research on "happiness" and found a lot of articles and 5-10 books in the field related to happiness and well-being.

One was *Buddha's Brain* by Rick Hanson, in which he investigated the brains of Buddhist monks using EEG and fMRI scans. It turned out that these monks were way off the scale in their capacity to generate positive emotions compared to the normal population. I thought that was interesting. I understood that the essence is a functional understanding of what is happening in our brains when we meditate. Then, I began to see what was in my surroundings and noticed a few things. I discovered a meditation center, linked to Buddhism, where people can meditate. I also came across the popular version of Buddhist meditation—mindfulness, which contains less mysticism. It is also easy to understand, and connects directly to what we do in everyday life. I have had an open approach, and tested a lot of different traditions. I have visited different centers, and I have gone on business mindfulness seminars and retreats.

You could say that I came into contact with mindfulness through the back door via meditation and Buddhism. I have done many other things to develop myself in terms of work, including presentation skills and how to act in a role, and how to be more efficient and productive, but I am impressed by the big effect that mindfulness has had in a relatively amount of short time.

In the summer of 2012, I started doing some research, but I hadn't actually meditated for more than six months. What I have mainly focused on is the awareness of the present moment, and the concentration exercises following the breath. Today, I meditate for 20 minutes a day with the help of a guided app. At the same time, I realize how little I know about how the mind works. I can only see the effect of my meditation, which is that I become aware of the inside and the outside—what I feel and think, and what I see and hear. That, in turn, creates an awareness of how I perceive others, how they express themselves and their facial expressions, and how that in itself creates more empathy and intuition.

I am able to apply many of these qualities to my work—for example intuition. I have had many years' experience in mathematics, science and logical thought. This is something that is promoted very strongly in the workplace because you always want to have logically framed arguments. Therefore, previously I based all problem-solving on rational thought and logic. Now, I use more intuition: how does this feel? Does this feel like the right thing to do? Is it really worthwhile? When you connect to your intuition, it becomes quicker to narrow down the problem area and discover the crux of the matter, and not just see the logic. Then, I can substantiate the feeling with logic and facts, where necessary. At first, I thought it was more risky to go on intuition, but since then I have noticed that it isn't at all. When I have used intuition, I have had more certainty. It is faster and more creative. The other route takes more time. One of our leaders advised me to use my intuition as much as possible, but I didn't know how until I started meditation.

I have also developed a more externally-oriented focus with more empathy. I think more about how I work, and imagine what it is like to be in that person's shoes. I work out what I need to do based on that person's perspective.

For example: today we had training in presentation skills. It was an instructor who ran the exercises with us, and one exercise was that I was meant to give a presentation with photos and role-playing. The person sitting opposite me was a hired actor, playing a client whom I would help. However, instead of sitting down and listening to the presentation, he came in and said that the work I had done was not good, and that all the errors were due to me and my team. Therefore, I wasn't making a presentation, but handling a disgruntled customer instead. Last year, I was more mechanical in my approach, and tried to convince him about what I wanted to talk about, and attempted to get him to listen to me by blocking what he wanted to talk about. However, this time I began to concentrate on the person I had in front of me, and became interested in how he thought and felt. He didn't want to talk about what I wanted, and I realized that we had to talk about what he was on about right now. I asked questions and listened actively, and I noticed his facial expression.

Being in the moment made all the difference. I hadn't done that before—on the contrary, I would often get feedback that I was lost in thought. Being present is something that I really have got the hang of since I started meditating. This is evident, especially in meetings. Nowadays, I turn off all forms of external stimuli. I turn off the computer and phone, and I don't take many notes. I listen actively, and when someone says something and makes a point, I acknowledge it to confirm that I have heard him/her. I ask quite a few questions and I listen for where this person is going with their comment. I also become aware of the underlying feeling when the person is speaking. Is this a concern, or is it quite neutral?

Being in the moment is possible with everything, and is perhaps most important in this whole process of change. Being present lays the foundation for being able to get into a flow, which has become central to everything I do, whether it is about writing emails, attending a meeting or writing a presentation. I have made the most progress in handling emails. I check my inbox two or three times per day, and when I write emails, I switch off everything else and concentrate completely on that.

However, today I discovered how many signals there are on my phone. The text and Facebook message alerts were audible and made me lose focus on what I was doing, even if it was only for a second or two, so I switched off all the notifications on the phone. I think that if someone sends me a text or Facebook message, it's not urgent, and if it is urgent, they will learn to call instead.

I don't want to shut myself off from the world, but just to disconnect from doing the things that I do automatically. Perhaps the time may come when it can buzz, and I don't lose focus—but I'm not there yet. When I hear the sound, I feel the urge to check what it is.

I can have fun in almost everything I do, when I focus on it completely. My ultimate goal is well-being and happiness, and everything leads in that direction. One way to make something fun is to focus on it fully; therefore, being present is essential.

Before, I had long checklists of things that I needed to remember to do. I thought in a mechanical and structured way, and didn't trust my mind to remember things. If someone asked me how the meeting went, I would say, "I'll just check my notes." Now, I have a new-found confidence that my mind can remember and sift through the information. If I'm calm, I will have full access to it, and then I can make more intelligent comments. I've even skipped all the lists I had inside my notebook, about what I should do during the day.

I believe that trust comes from mindfulness training. I was on a ten-day Vipassana retreat, where we meditated from morning to night. It was a silent retreat, and you don't look at each other—there are no external stimuli. I was able to delve deep into myself and when I meditated, many interesting things came up—a lot to add to my "to-do list" that I was going to write down as soon as I could. What happened instead was that I began to trust that the thoughts would come back if they were important enough. Mentally, I put them aside, until the day came when I was allowed to talk and write again. I still do this. Now, I know that I will have access to ideas and thoughts later, if I only trust that my mind is working.

Another result from the intense meditation retreat was that I can now tell the difference when I have full access to my mind, and when it has contracted, and I'm in a fight-or-flight mood. When the mind is in overdrive, I feel that it's not functioning optimally, and then I relax it. It's like using the clutch while driving a car—you don't accelerate or brake. My perspective returns and my thoughts go from black-and-white to more nuanced shades.

The main part of my work is giving advice, and my mind is my tool, so it needs to be in good shape. Before, I used to be in overdrive, going from meeting to meeting, and I would mentally wind up before a meeting. It didn't work very well. Now, I de-stress the mind instead for a while before meetings. It's actually in two stages. The first is to get the mind in a better state, in which I can think clearly, and the other is to get into focus just before the meeting. Walking between the buildings where I work, gives me that opportunity. I can either go out and think lots of thoughts, or I can go and appreciate that I am out walking and look around and get some fresh air. The latter gives me a mental break.

In summary, my internal characteristics or qualities that have changed are intuition, empathy, presence and an awareness of balance in the mind. It is easy to connect balance to meditation, because both are training concentration and focus, but also relaxation. I can imagine that it makes many people more persistent, and not so moody. I haven't noticed that much myself because I have always been quite calm. However, I have gone from being very logically driven to being more empathetic. That has had a dramatic effect on my values. It's like I had a huge muscle on only one side of the brain, and now I'm beginning to discover that I have another equally large muscle on the other side. This has raised questions about my values.

Personally, it has meant that I socialize more now with close friends and family. I have become more altruistic. At home, I have collected bags of things that I'm going to give away, because I think that someone else might need them. I have never been materialistic and have become much less materialistic lately because I do not feel attached to things. I don't buy anything else apart from necessities like food and clothing. People in Stockholm think it's great fun to talk about apartments, and that makes me a little worried about people's values in general.

However, I would say that the effects of mindfulness are more noticeable in micro-moments, often in a subtle way, rather than in a big dramatic way. For example, I might notice that someone is in a certain mood, perhaps a bit worse than usual, or it might even be me. It was like that the other morning when I came in to work—I felt that I was a bit down, so I played a song I like. I only listened for about two to three minutes, but it made a difference. It wasn't a result of habitually playing music, but it was the awareness that my mood was below par and I needed to do something about it.

There are many small things and situations where it feels good to be aware of what is happening to others and myself, and what I appreciate in everyday life. You get a different focus on what contributes to your overall well-being. From the outside, there probably isn't much difference. It's not like having a hair-cut, and suddenly you have a new hairstyle, but for me there's a dramatic difference."

For Carl, mindfulness and meditation have been a way to search for (and find, in part) what is important in life—the elusive concept of happiness. What is particularly interesting with Carl in this context is that his shift of perspective in life towards compassion and altruism hasn't affected his ability to be productive and effective at work—rather the opposite. When Carl began training the ability to maintain a relaxed focus and listen to his intuition, he felt that he really became effective and, as a result, more productive. Therefore, he had no problem "stepping down" from his old job and "just" working 50-55 hours a week, which he does today.

For many people, however, the words *"productivity"* and *"efficiency"* are loaded with negative connotations. These words makes you think of stressed caregivers in home care services that run from one patient to the next, out of breath, with barely the time to say, "Hello, how are you today?"; or workplaces with ever shortening deadlines and rationalizing coffee breaks, and where people would cough nervously at the question whether there is room for reflection and thoughtfulness.

Paul Gilbert, a professor of psychology, describes the strong links between the high value our society places on efficiency and increasing psychological suffering, in his book The Compassionate Mind. He believes that our quest for ever-increasing productivity and efficiency has direct repercussions on stress and burnout, which affect many in the workplace.

However, without ignoring the sometimes overwhelming demands of knowledge workers today—let's look at what "efficient" and "effective" actually mean. "Effective" means something produces the desired result. "Efficient" means that the results are achieved with minimal effort.

To be effective, therefore, means to produce what is desirable. There is an aspect of quality as well as quantity. If we are effective, we get a lot done and what we do meets high standards. At the same time, to be efficient means using as little energy and effort as possible to produce a specific result.

Therefore, to be effective and efficient means that you get more done in less time, of a higher quality and, perhaps most importantly, with less effort. Given this, why would we not want to strive to be as efficient and effective as possible? What is the point of doing things in a way that means that it takes longer, has a worse result and requires more effort? The more efficient we are, the more time we release. The more effective we are, the more we can relax and put our energy on the right things.

- Efficiency and effectiveness: the ability to do things with less effort and in less time.
- Productivity: The ability to contribute as much as possible.

This is what impact you can have on an inner level, within yourself. Efficiency and effectiveness lead to productivity.

In the previous chapter, we discussed the importance of being in touch with our values. We also saw that when we really come into contact with what we value, it often results in living meaningful lives, where we are actually able to contribute something. Our time on this planet is short. If we have come into contact with our deepest values and seen that we want to do something that is meaningful and can contribute to others and the world we live in, why wouldn't we want to be as productive as possible? The clearer our values are, the more interested we become in not wasting any time or energy on anything that is not in line with these values. We want to be as efficient as possible in relation to what we value.

This can be illustrated with an example from my own life (Martin): right now, my overall goal is to spread mindfulness to as many people as possible. The reason for this is that I am convinced that it can give people the tools to live more relaxed, joyful and productive lives. Most of my time (80 per cent) at the moment is spent doing lectures, mindfulness training and individual counseling with business clients. At the same time, I am working with Jon Kabat-Zinn (one of the world's leading experts on mindfulness) to develop mindfulness apps for mobile phones, and with the Potential Project to develop a global online learning center for corporate-based mindfulness training. And, of course I am writing this book.

In addition,, I'm a husband and father, and the time I spend with my family is sacred. I never work past 5 p.m. When I am with my wife and daughter, I give them 100 per cent of my attention and, therefore, basically never work in the evenings or on weekends.

As a result, I need to be productive to reach my goals. To succeed with that and at the same time feel calm, unstressed and happy, I definitely need to be as efficient as possible. The key to this is focus and presence. The agent is mindfulness training. This entails the following:

- When I meet a client individually, I am 100 per cent focused and present. It is not possible to be empathetic and really understand the suffering someone is experiencing if I am not present mentally.
- When I am lecturing or leading a group, I am 100 per cent focused and present. The difference between an okay lecture and a fantastic lecture is to be really absorbed in the delivery.
- If I have a maximum of one hour available every day to write the book, I do that, and only that, during the time allocated.

- When I'm talking about something important with my wife, or playing with my daughter, I let go of all the thoughts about clients, writing books and app development.

RELAXATION AND DIRECTED ATTENTION

One of the world's foremost experts in training focused attention is B. Alan Wallace. He has studied these practices for more than 40 years, and devotes all his time to lecturing, and teaching meditation and mindfulness training. He is also the initiator of Shamatha Project, one of the most ambitious research projects on the effects of mindfulness training that has been conducted.

In the Shamatha Project, a large team of scientists investigated people who participated in a three-month, intensive retreat, in which the participants practiced mindfulness, focusing on directed attention for up to 12 hours each day. Wallace was the one who was responsible for and led the mindfulness training.

At one point, he was asked to name the three most important aspects of focus training. Without hesitation, he replied, "The most important aspect is relaxation. This is followed by relaxation, and after that is relaxation." Therefore, a fully focused mind is, according to Wallace, a completely relaxed mind.

For most of us, this may sound very strange. We are accustomed to using a lot of effort to focus. This was the same for Carl during his time in the large consulting firm, and for everyone who is untrained. The more focused we are, and the longer we are focused, the more mentally and physically exhausted we become. This has been measured.

There is one test, in which participants have to keep their attention on a computer screen where letters are flashing by in rapid succession. If an "X" appears, the participants press a key, and if there is another letter, they don't press it. The test lasts 20 minutes and afterwards the participants are almost always completely exhausted.

The reason it requires such a big effort for a relatively simple challenge, is that we are unaccustomed to directing our attention. In the same way as everything else that we haven't practiced, directed attention requires a large amount of energy. Consequently, all other activities based on the ability of directed attention also take a lot of energy. However, the more we practice, the more natural and effortless it becomes for us to maintain our focus on something.

How can this be linked to efficiency? We achieve maximum efficiency when we can be as relaxed as possible. Maximum efficiency is about doing exactly what is needed—and nothing else. If the task you want to perform requires directed attention (which most tasks do) and you don't have the ability to maintain focus on something without great exertion, then you will automatically use up energy unnecessarily. Everyone who has crashed on the couch, totally exhausted after a hard day at work, knows what it feels like to perform tasks in a way that leaves us mentally exhausted.

WE ARE NOT AS EFFECTIVE AS WE THINK

Gloria Mark, PhD, of the University of California, examined how often we are interrupted during the workday. Mark and her colleagues conducted a study with 36 office workers. They made note of all the work activities of the participants every single second for three days. It turned out that the average time people worked on a task before they were interrupted was three minutes and five seconds. In addition, it was found that 44 per cent of the interruptions were internal, in other words, not caused by external distractions, but by the people themselves, in the form of thoughts and impulses.

Maybe you have the feeling that you often get disturbed by phone calls, emails and colleagues, but the fact is that you interrupt yourself as much as you are interrupted by other people and things.

However, it is possible to influence the amount of external distractions. We can restrict the number of times a day we check our email, as Carl did. We can turn off the mobile notifications, and if we are lucky, maybe we can even close our office door. In some workplaces, where people sit in open offices, they have experimented with putting small flags on the desk, where a green flag means "you may disturb me" and a red flag means "do not disturb." A project manager with a glass office told me how she often sat with a mobile earpiece in her ear, whether she was on a call or not, to signal to colleagues that she was busy and, therefore, did not want to be disturbed. However, nifty and useful these tricks are, interruptions in our modern working life are more or less inevitable.

What is interesting in this context is that we are causing half of the interruptions ourselves. Suppose you have decided to set aside two hours to write an important report. During that time, you will interrupt yourself at least twelve times, according to Gloria Mark's conclusions. Various studies provide slightly different information on how long it takes from the break until you return to the original task, but let us use a low number, and assume that it takes four minutes. Twelve interruptions means, that during the 120 minutes you set aside for the report, 48 minutes were taken up by distractions that you yourself have caused.

Let's look at that again: when you had planned to focus on something for two hours, in actuality, you wasted three quarters of an hour on your own distractions.

Almost half of the interruptions are internal, which means you could almost double your efficiency if you had full control of your focused attention!

To summarize and simplify the causal chain, you can say that the more aware you are of your task, the more relaxed you will be—which in turn leads to both higher efficiency and less fatigue.

Two rules for mental efficiency
- Focus on what you choose to focus on.
- Consciously choose if you want to engage with a distraction.

DOING THE RIGHT THINGS

In 1906, the Italian economist Vilfredo Pareto observed that 80 per cent of all the land in Italy was owned by 20 per cent of the population. He also noted that 20 per cent of the pea shells in his garden contained 80 per cent of the peas. On the basis of these observations, management consultant Joseph M. Juran formulated what he called the Pareto principle. He said that in many contexts, 80 per cent of the results come from 20 per cent of the causes. In the business context, this means that 80 per cent of revenue comes from 20 per cent of the activities that a company engages in.

On a personal level, it means that 80 per cent of everything you accomplish comes from 20 per cent of your efforts.

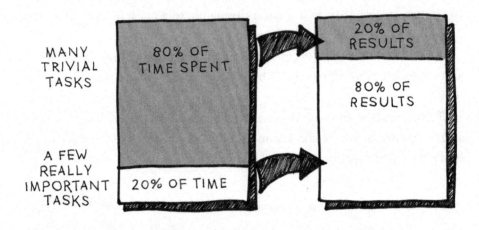

At any given moment, there is always an almost infinite amount of actions we could do. The question is how to decide which of these are worthy of our time and attention. We often confuse being busy with being productive. It's easy to feel like you are getting a lot done just because you constantly have a lot of activities going on, and are running from one to the next. However, if the Pareto principle is correct (and it is for most people) you should actually be able to ignore 80 per cent of what you do, and still only be 20 per cent less productive. Conversely, if you really learned to prioritize properly, you could quadruple your productivity without having to exert yourself any more.

To be able to determine what you should do at every moment, we suggest you follow the steps in the process shown on the next page.

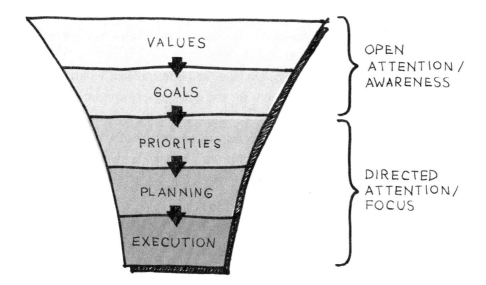

Values: As we saw in the last chapter, it is extremely important that you be in touch with your values. It's your values that give direction to your life.

Goals: when you are clear on your values, you can use them to formulate goals. With the help of your goals, you can control your own behavior based on a short- and medium-term perspective.

Priorities: once you have clear goals, you can begin to prioritize the activities that are important. If you know what you want to achieve, it is easier to act in accordance with the Pareto principle—you choose the 20 per cent of what you do that will give you 80 per cent of the effect.

Planning: once you have prioritized the activities that are most important, you can plan them. Instead of being constantly reactive and just acting according to what turns up in the moment, you can create an overview and space for what you know is favorable in the long term. If you don't plan important activities, something else will always come in between.

Implementation: the last step is to carry out the activities according to your plan. At this point, it is important to keep complete focus on one activity at a time. You can be relaxed and confident in doing the right thing at every moment because you have planned what to do, based on a priority that is in line with your goals and overall values.

As you can see in the diagram, each step in the process is supported by mindfulness. The more aware you become, i.e. the more you train the ability of open attention, the more you can get in touch with and clarify your core values. The same awareness also helps you formulate and define your goals. Training in directed, focused attention will then help you prioritize, plan and carry out the right activities.

When reality changes—as it always does—open, receptive attention will help you correct your direction, for example, by reformulating your priorities, if necessary.

In Chapter 10, where we briefly present the structure of a mindfulness training program, there are practical tips on how you can work with goal setting, prioritizing and planning.

The ability of directed attention is the prerequisite to enable you to change your brain (and yourself) in the way you want.

CHAPTER 7

TRAIN YOUR BRAIN!

HOW MINDFULNESS CAUSES NEUROLOGICAL CHANGE

IMAGINE A PERSON WITH A SHORT FUSE. We can call him Ellis. He is 30 years old, often touchy and is prone to yelling at colleagues. Ellis usually swears at the photocopier when it malfunctions, and is often seen fuming and stomping through the office with a furrowed brow and clenched jaw muscles. It is often a bit uncomfortable to meet Ellis, because you never really know what mood he is in.

Only twenty years ago, psychologists and brain scientists agreed that this was Ellis. In those days, it was believed that the personality was fully developed sometime in the late teens, and that the brain developed until about the age of 25. After that, it remained as it was, or got worse. It was believed that brain cells gradually die as we become older and more sluggish. People could possibly speed up the process using alcohol and drugs (which we certainly can, but we can also do completely the opposite). It was believed that the personality and brain had completely developed after reaching adulthood. With regard to Ellis, he would simply be a person with a short fuse and would remain so for life. End of story.

Modern brain research shows that this is not true. Over the last two decades, scientists have discovered that the brain is far more flexible and malleable than previously thought. Scientists call this neuroplasticity. It is no small discovery. Today, we have an entirely different understanding of a short fuse, and the opportunity for change. What actually happens when Ellis feels mistreated by a colleague (or a photocopier) is that part of his brain—the limbic system—perceives this treatment as a real threat, and responds with an aggressive impulse. It could be said that Ellis is kidnapped by this impulse, and reacts automatically with anger. However, it is not necessary for him to do this. Ellis can act differently by strengthening his prefrontal cortex, the anterior part of the brain that controls attention and executive functions. Such training would help him notice the impulses from the limbic system, without letting them control his behavior. In the beginning this would be difficult, and would require a lot of conscious focus. However, every time Ellis manages to remain with the emotional impulse without reacting, he is gradually reprogramming his own brain. New neural connections are created and, in time, certain parts of his brain structure will be strengthened and begin to dominate other parts. This results in a longer "fuse" and a personality change for Ellis.

THE BRAIN SCAN ERA

For over two thousand years, people who engaged in mental training claimed similar changes—that meditation has influenced how they approach the environment. They have testified to improved well-being and performance, with a clear and calm state of mind. And, in this book, many managers and employees give examples of how mindfulness has improved their focus and performance, as well as making their lives happier and more meaningful.

That these changes hadn't been validated by neuroscience until the late 1990s, has to do with brain imaging technology. It was only in this decade that fMRI and MRI cameras were refined to such a degree that neuroscientists could actually compare personal statements to what they could observe. These observations have been done (and continue to be done) in two ways: by identifying in which centre of the brain the activity is taking place and by measuring the structure of the cortex (the 1.5-5-mm thick mass covering the rest of the brain like a walnut-shaped grey blanket, where neurons carry information to each other).

Research based on brain scan technology is presented almost daily at universities and hospitals around the world. Most studies are carried out on people with mental health problems or healthy mindfulness practitioners, and the results are not directly linked to working life. Nevertheless, the findings are of great importance regarding how we are managing at work, and now brain researchers have shown that mindfulness training leads to:

- Enhanced attention
- Increased compassion
- Improved short-term memory
- A less distracted mind
- Better conflict resolution
- A greater level of cognitive control.

These results elucidate two fundamental differences in the brains of people who practice mindfulness compared to others. Those who practice mindfulness have:

1. Increased activity and structure in the front of the brain, the prefrontal cortex (PFC). This contains the ability to focus, make informed decisions and regulate emotions.
2. Less activity in the default mode network (DMN), a set of networks in the brain that are active when we don't have a specific task to focus on. DMN is spread over several parts of the brain, and its activity corresponds to distraction, automated behavior and self-referential processes.

Let us take a closer look at the DMN, since activity in this area is the phenomenon that knowledge workers seem to suffer from most of all these days—a fragmented and randomly functioning brain.

Matt Killingsworth and Dan Gilbert, two researchers at Harvard University, have studied the consequences of a distracted mind. In their study, A Wandering Mind is an Unhappy Mind, they tested the hypothesis that an unhappy mind arises because we often find ourselves mentally somewhere other than where we are physically and geographically. In fact, the research duo says that thoughts "about something else" occupy about half our waking hours!

The fact that we even have this ability could possibly be understood from an evolutionary perspective. One can imagine that the capacity to focus on a life far away from the place where people find themselves - in memories and in the future, in relationships and self-image - has contributed to the ability to adjust to new life circumstances. However, in modern working life the wandering mind, which usually takes place unconsciously, results in a number of negative consequences. It may, of course, be quite dangerous to think of other things when driving a truck or operating on someone's kidneys, but also in less risky jobs, wandering thoughts generally have a negative impact on work performance. The distracted mind has even become such a common problem that it is now classified as a neurological condition - ADT (attention deficit trait).

It was the psychiatrist Edward M. Hallowell who named the condition after 25 years of treating patients with ADHD (attention-deficit/hyperactivity disorder). He discovered that more and more clients who did not have the genetic component that is present in ADHD, showed similar symptoms. ADT arises then as a result of environmental influences and our inability to manage them.

Hallowell describes the effect like a huge tidal wave of stimuli that are increasingly vying for our attention and time. At the same time, our mind is filled with constant noise and gradually loses its ability to pay full attention to anything. This inability causes people to feel constantly guilty, become mentally absent and experience surreptitious feelings of panic. In order to master the situation, most people try to pretend that everything is fine, by making an all-out effort. However, under the façade, stress and lack of focus increase, which in turn have long-term consequences in terms of illness and reduced performance.

Self-reference – a screen between you and reality

The DMN also plays a central role in self-referential thoughts. If you have high activity in the DMN, you will be more aware of the concept of yourself than of your direct experience.

Self-reference is the way you describe yourself, and it is usually positively or negatively charged, for example, "I am an honest boss. I am clever. I have integrity." Or, "I am an inadequate boss. I am stupid. My co-workers do not trust me." Each time you return to this type of conceptualization, your DMN is activated.

This self-referencing affects both your work performance and the quality of your relationships. For example, if you are thinking more about how the manager is perceiving you than on the presentation you are giving, then the result will not be as good as if you undertook your task whole-heartedly.

It has been found that the activity that is linked to self-referencing has stopped or decreased significantly in the brains of mindfulness practitioners. This means that instead of interpreting events through the grid of preconceived notions about yourself, you see each experience as unique, and as it actually is, based on your impressions.

Neuroscience research shows that mindfulness:
- Strengthens the structure of the PFC
- Reduces or stops activity in the DMN
- Strengthens the structure of the TPJ
- Increases the initial activity in the ACC, which gradually decreases
- Reduces activity in the amygdala
- Strengthens the structure of and reduces activity in the PCC
- Strengthens the structure of the hippocampus.

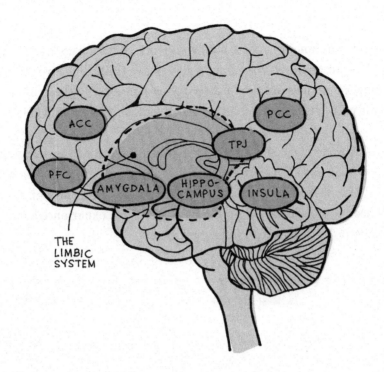

The prefrontal cortex (PFC) – the centre for executive functions such as planning, decision making and evaluation.

The anterior cingulate cortex (ACC) – part of the PFC, the centre of attention and emotional regulation.

The limbic system—the brain's emotional centre—is activated during stress. Behavior is controlled by our desire to avoid discomfort and seek pleasure.

The amygdala – part of the limbic system, where emotional reactions and internal stress occurs. Memory is also processed here.

The hippocampus – part of the limbic system and the centre of learning and memory processing. It converts short-term memory into long-term memory storage in other parts of the brain. This is the only part of the brain that can produce new cells.

The temporal-parietal junction (TPJ) – the centre of empathy and compassion.

The default mode network (DMN) – a neural network spread across the brain associated with the wandering mind, habitual behavior, "autopilot" and self-referential processes.

The posterior cingulate cortex (PCC) – part of the DMN. It is the key to understanding the context and relevance of our impressions

The PFC – your friend in the fight against distractions

The PFC is the centre of our executive functions: the ability to separate conflicting thoughts, evaluate the consequences of our decisions, set goals and regulate emotions. It is also the part of the brain that developed later during human evolution. The PFC constitutes only 4-5 per cent of total brain volume, but without it we would not cope very well. We would not be able to get to work, follow a recipe, create a video game or find the Higgs particle. The PFC is also the only place in the brain where we think thoughts that don't come from external sources or from our senses. We can consciously create thoughts ourselves in the PFC, and this is where we are able to think about our thoughts, feelings and behaviors.

The ability to focus on what we believe is most favorable for ourselves and others is located in the PFC. When we strengthen the PFC, which we do with mindfulness, we become more prone to acting consciously, rather than reacting impulsively based on our DMN and our emotionally-driven limbic system.

Several studies have also observed increased activity in the centre of attention—the anterior cingulate cortex (ACC), which is a specific part of the PFC—of mindfulness practitioners, compared to people who do not practice mindfulness.

Create your own structure, create new cells and live longer!

It is possible to pick up the pieces of a fragmented mind. If you change your behavior by deliberately focusing on certain aspects of the world around you, the corresponding areas of the brain will grow stronger and begin to dominate other areas of the brain. It is not only the prefrontal cortex where you can stimulate growth, but you can also influence the conditions for the formation of new brain cells.

The hippocampus—the place where short-term memories are transformed into long-term memories—is the only part of the brain that can produce new cells. When your inner stress system is activated, the breeding ground for the formation of new cells is inhibited, but the opposite occurs during mindfulness training. Neuroscientist Sara Lazar of Harvard Medical School discovered that the structure of the hippocampus grows in connection with mindfulness training. Mindfulness, therefore, appears to counteract the destructive effects that stress causes, and instead creates the conditions for the formation of new cells.

Even chromosomes react to what we are doing. A new field of brain research focuses on telomeres, which are the part of chromosomes affecting life span. The hypothesis is: the shorter the telomeres, the shorter the life span. A research team led by Elissa Epel, a professor of psychiatry at Yale University, have discovered that these microscopic chromosome parts change as a result of mindfulness training. People who meditate regularly have longer telomeres than others, which is believed to have a direct impact on life expectancy. How much longer we live has not yet been determined.

Neuroscience shows us that if we learn to train our brain the right way, we improve our attention, compassion and short-term memory and reduce the wandering mind. We also create the conditions for new cell formation and a longer life!

DIRECTING YOUR OWN BRAIN

Directed attention is the very condition for you to be able to change your brain (and all of you) in the way you want. If you direct your attention to a particular activity on a daily basis, then the corresponding part of the brain literally becomes larger. This process is described by the phrase, "What fires together, wires together," coined by the neuropsychologist Donald Hebb. If you direct your attention in a certain way, the corresponding neurons are activated ("fired"), and intertwined to form new connections in the brain structure ("wired").

There are several studies that have mapped how directed attention has left an imprint on and literally transformed the brain. For example, in a study of professional musicians who turned their attention to practicing an instrument for a considerable number of hours, they had significantly more grey matter in the parts that constitute the centre of musicality. Similarly, it has been seen how London's taxi drivers have a greatly enlarged cortex in the parts corresponding to the centre of spatial ability.

Transferring this to mindfulness training, when we place the attention back to the present and on the breath again and again with perseverance, this gradually alters the cascade of corresponding brain activity. The new activity patterns are coded differently than if had we engaged in random behavior. In this way, the structure of the brain is changed, which in turn will affect behavior. This is how habits are formed, and that is why it will be easier the fiftieth time you sit down to play the piano or practice mindfulness than the first.

These changes also appear to be sustainable over time, even if mental training, in the same way as physical exercise, is partly perishable. You cannot immunize yourself against future fragmentation and unconscious behavior by practicing mindfulness for three months and then stop. The neurons will then gradually lose connection with each other, and the old habits will eventually return.

Thicker cortex = less effort

Scientists have found various changes in the brains of long-term meditating Tibetan monks and novice mindfulness practitioners. The monks showed lower activity in the ACC (which controls attention) than in beginners, who had quite high activity in this area.

The difference can be explained by the fact that the more time you have spent practicing mindfulness, the less effort is needed to be able to direct your attention. Conversely, you initially need to make quite a lot of effort to maintain focus (which can be useful information for those who want to start practicing mindfulness).

Another study measured the activity and structure of a neighbor of the ACC, the posterior cingulate cortex (PCC), which plays a central role in understanding context and how relevant sensory impressions are to the self. You would anticipate the activity to be high in mindfulness practitioners, but the results were the same as for the monks in the aforementioned study. The PCC remained inactive for twenty experienced mindfulness practitioners versus the control group. In contrast, the brain structure of the PCC in the mindfulness group was significantly stronger.

It may sound paradoxical, but this can be explained by the fact that a previously high activity in the area has built up a strong brain structure that has eventually taken over the function that the activity previously had. Translated into human behavior, this means that after serious training, you will be able to act consciously, without having to strain yourself in the least.

MORE REGULATION OF EMOTIONS!

If you ask people who practice mindfulness to identify the biggest change they are experiencing, one of the most common answers is "peace"—that they now feel more peace of mind. In neuroplastic terms, peace is the ability to regulate emotions in a way that makes you feel more in control. For example, Gitte Matzen, in chapter 2, says mindfulness training taught her to find and maintain her distance from strong feelings that had previously controlled her behavior in an unconscious and sometimes destructive way.

What has happened in Gitte's brain is that she has strengthened her PFC and at the same time lowered the activity in the DMN, which contributes to her ability to pay attention to and relate constructively to her emotions.

A study in 2005 found some interesting changes in the brain linked to emotional regulation. A research team studied the cortical thickness of twenty mindfulness practitioners versus a control group, and found that the grey matter of the practitioners was thicker in all investigated regions, of the brain except one. The grey matter was significantly less in the amygdala—a small kernel in the limbic system, which is the centre for fear and internal stress, among other things.

This result was found by the research group after only eight weeks of mindfulness training. Apart from the mindfulness training, nothing else in the participants' lives had changed. They still had the same stressful jobs and they were still living with the same annoying people around them. The reduced size of the amygdala showed that their relationship with the environment had changed in two months. They experienced significantly less fear, anxiety and worry.

Another study found that the participants, who were experienced mindfulness practitioners, had developed increased activity in the anterior insula, an area associated with how we respond to pain and other emotions. The result is believed to reflect the increased ability of experienced meditators to be aware of how different sorts of feelings come and go, without letting these emotions overtake them.

However, this enhanced capacity to regulate your emotions does not mean that you become emotionally numb after mindfulness training. On the contrary—the study by Lazar also showed how the cortex in the temporal-parietal junction (TPJ), the centre of empathy and compassion, had become stronger.

In chapter 6, Carl explained how this can manifest itself at work. When he received the highest rating in the evaluation of a staged meeting with a difficult customer, he attributed the outcome to his increased capacity for empathy, "Last year I was more mechanical in my approach, and tried to convince him what I wanted to talk about, and tried to get him on my track by blocking what he wanted to talk about. This time, I began to concentrate on the person I had in front of me, and became interested in how he thought and felt. ...I asked questions and listened actively, and I noticed his facial expressions. Being present made all the difference."

The evolution of emotions

Paul Gilbert, professor of clinical psychology, has been studying the brain from an evolutionary perspective, and argues that our brain, or more specifically, our emotional regulatory system, has lagged behind the development of society and fallen out of step with our time. According to Gilbert, human beings are essentially controlled by two regulatory systems derived from a bygone era, when we lived on the savannah.

One is an alert system linked to fear and anger, which was a successful survival tool when there was rustling in the bushes, and we connected this to a lion trying to eat us. The warning system triggers feelings of anger and fear—which in turn prepares us for fight or flight.

The second of the brain's emotional control systems is the source of emotions such as arousal and pleasure. It is a system that makes us interested in food, friends, sexual partners, money and career, and which helps us discover and become interested in acquiring resources to survive and thrive. This system has a survival function to ensure reproduction.

The problem, according to Gilbert, is that both of these systems nowadays often end up in conflict with the capacity of the PFC to plan and take perspective, which developed much later in evolutionary history. Today it is rarely necessary to run for our life when there is rustling in the bushes, so Gilbert suggests that we need to train an updated version of emotional control.

He calls the third system contentment- and compassion-focused emotional regulation. It is linked to feelings of contentment in situations where we are neither threatened nor aim to achieve the things we want. It is a source of feelings such as well-being, safety and belonging.

It appears that mindfulness training leads us from the first two systems to the third. To feel contented, secure and belonging – or at peace—are now basic skills in a working environment that is becoming more challenging with increasing demands and tighter deadlines.

TIPS

Scan your own brain!

Go back to the open attention exercise in chapter 4. It gives you the opportunity to observe your brain activity without an fMRI scanner. Instead of letting yourself be hijacked by thoughts, feelings and impulses, you can observe them neutrally. Try to be like a scientist exploring your own experience with curiosity.

You can practice on yourself when a strong feeling arises, for example when you feel anger at an annoying colleague. This anger arises automatically in one part of your brain, and it doesn't help to try to push it away, it may even make things worse.

Instead, use your brain's ability to observe your emotional state. By practicing on yourself in this way, that is to notice when anger arises— and even put a label on it ("I am starting to feel annoyed")—so you will be quicker to notice when emotions such as anger arise. Then, you will have time to shift your attention to something else you would like to focus on, for example the task you have in front of you, which prevents emotions from building up and taking over. This is how you can regulate your limbic system and keep in touch with your PFC.

Eight weeks make a difference

Research shows that regular mindfulness training transforms your brain in the regions that are important for emotional regulation, empathy, decision-making and self-referential processes. Thicker grey matter in the PFC and stunted activity in the DMN make you more focused, efficient, empathetic and less self-centered. These changes have been measured in mindfulness practitioners and other meditators after eight weeks of training.

Hard to remember?

The memory problems that we often experience, when we are stressed and our attention is divided, are closely linked to the difficulty focusing our attention. You could even say that they are the same thing.

Working memory has been defined by some researchers as the ability to maintain and manage the information that is relevant to the goal, without being distracted. Therefore, one can say that working memory is the very ability to control our attention.

"Creativity is the central source of meaning in our lives."

Mihaly Csikszentmihalyi

CHAPTER 8

THE JOURNALIST WHO DISCOVERED HER GUT FEELING

HOW MINDFULNESS IS RELATED TO CREATIVITY AND INNOVATION

It is only when we have woken up that we realize how much of our lives that we actually slept through.
Ellen J. Langer, Professor of Psychology at
Harvard University

FREELANCE JOURNALIST ANNETTE WALLQVIST EXPERIENCED what she called "the fast years" early in the new millennium. She took all the assignments she could get, delivered them as promised, and went from strength to strength. She was a high flyer with many clients and a big salary. This lasted for three to four years, then Annette began to experience the symptoms of stress. Mindfulness was recommended, and Annette felt disheartened, because she had done a meditation course in the past and thought it was all incredibly boring. "I thought that mindfulness would be the same, but I didn't have much to lose."

Admittedly, the mindfulness course included the seated meditation that Annette didn't like, although when the positive effect slowly became apparent, it overcame her resistance to what eventually turned out to be not so boring after all.

Step by step, and with daily training, her stress levels began to drop, and Annette was surprised by the changes that began to permeate her life. The most unexpected was that she developed the capacity to listen to her children in a way she had not done previously. In relation to her work, Annette describes how she began to adopt a more creative approach. She began to choose assignments based on her own interests, and started playing more with the text. If she had previously had quite a clear angle on a job and mainly set out to get the "right" wording, now she began to allow herself to start a creative process, which meant playing more with uncertainty and feeling her way.

"Today, I went to a seminar on women's rights issues. It covered a very wide range of topics, and I feel that it'll be difficult to write an article about the seminar, as intended. However, I got an idea that I intend to show the editor. There was a very interesting speaker, and I think I can make her the focal point. It will be something completely different than what was intended, but probably more interesting, with a better result."

Another example Annette gives is when she went to Reykjavik to write a travel story. Annette wasn't particularly fond of the city, and she was wondering how to write an article good enough to publish, when she discovered silversmiths on every other block. Annette, who is very fond of arts and crafts, let her curiosity and gut feeling take over, and linked the story to Iceland's rich silversmith culture. The result was a different article than planned, and Annette felt very happy with it.

When the seasoned freelance journalist talks about how mindfulness has led to changing her attitude, she occasionally places her hand over her stomach, and says she feels more centered and less judgmental of herself now that she is brave enough to use more of her own reflections in her articles. "I'm no longer afraid to be mundane."

Annette tells us that another change is that she takes more time to write an article now, because she thinks it is so pleasurable and such fun. When asked whether the change has had any negative aspects, she thinks for a moment and then says with a laugh that makes it difficult to determine whether she is serious or not. "Well, the customer list has shrunk. I make slightly less money now than in the past, and I've begun to wonder whether it soon might be time not to have as much fun!"

Many believe that creativity is something that a select group of people are born with, like a gift from heaven. We are happy to label particularly outstanding people who express themselves creatively as "geniuses," and we believe that they can achieve great things without much effort. We assume that creativity is about expressing yourself artistically' therefore writers, directors and composers are creative by definition—but a journalist? Well, maybe. What about an insurance officer? No. Or, maybe...?

FROM WHAT YOU DO, TO HOW YOU DO IT.

In a famous psychological experiment, children were allowed to paint freely without instructions and evaluation. These children saw themselves as artists and continued to paint on their own. They seemed to have found their own motivation and desire to express themselves. Children in another group who also painted, received repeated reviews of their efforts. Even when the evaluations were positive, these children gradually stopped taking the initiative to paint.

Eleanor Rosch, Professor of Psychology at Berkeley University, refers to the experiment as proof that we all have creativity within us that we have been in contact with at some time in our lives, but at some stage, something happens to inhibit it. What happens, according to Rosch, is that we learn to consider the results in a judgmental way, instead of concentrating on the creative process. She points out that it is not necessary for the painting itself to give rise to the actual creativity, but the approach that we have to the task, no matter what the content. This approach varies, depending on where we are in the creative process, but the point remains, and she emphasizes each word:

– It's about how we do something, not what we do.

Ellen J. Langer, Professor of Psychology at Harvard University, is on the same track. She is convinced that we all have a creative nature that may manifest itself in our daily life in everything we do, based on how we do it: our culture, our language and our most mundane activities. It is when we turn on the autopilot and act unconsciously that we lose creativity. In that way, she says, mindfulness is both a prerequisite and a synonym for creativity. Langer chooses not to distinguish between the two concepts. She talks about mindful creativity, an approach to life that all of us can practice.

Eleanor Rosch tells of a woman who did just that. She delivered the mail for many years and was dying of boredom from the predictable daily routines and by her behavior on autopilot.

"Instead of going mad or resigning, she decided to really notice everything that she saw during her rounds and to actually take in what was happening along the path where she had been thousands and thousands of times. She began to see children playing in their front yards. She calmed down barking dogs and she stayed and talked with the people who came out to retrieve their mail. This creative approach saved her sanity."

Whether or not the mail delivery person was able to get "full-blast living" from her new approach is unclear, but these are the words that psychologist and author Mihaly Csikszentmihalyi uses when he describes what a person can really be with creativity. He believes that creativity is the closest state to giving us the full satisfaction we all hope to get out of life. Moreover, creativity provides the foundation of all innovation. Csikszentmihalyi, who coined the related term "flow"" does not mince words in his book, *Creativity,* when he summarizes the essence of the interviews he made with 91 creative people about their development, drive and creativity. "Creativity is the central source of meaning in our life. Most things that are interesting, important and human are the result of creativity. What separates us from the apes—our language, values, artistic expression, scientific understanding and technology—is the result of individual ingenuity that has been recognized, rewarded and put forward through learning."

From this perspective, creativity can be seen as both an attitude we can all learn, which brings meaning and satisfaction to our lives, and as a prerequisite to achieve interesting and important results—we can call it innovation.

Already in 1942, the economist Joseph Schumpeter reasoned that creativity was the soul of economic development. He meant that the process of creativity leads to innovation, which in turn can change everything, from how people think to how entire organizations and societies evolve. His ideas were ahead of their time and had to be mothballed during industrialism. Now we have caught up with Schumpeter, and in our times of uncertainty about how to deal with mass unemployment and economic imbalances, an increasing number of business leaders, community developers and economists are using his ideas.

For example, David Ahlstrom, Professor of Economics, says that the goal of a modern business must be "to develop new and innovative products and services that generate economic growth while contributing benefits to the community." Professor Michael Porter agrees, "Innovation is the core issue for economic success." When we see the innovative success of companies like Google, Apple, Amazon, Microsoft and IBM, it is difficult to argue with that. When a number of IBM business executives in 2010 ranked the qualities they believed to be the most crucial for future leaders, creativity came in first place.

Therefore, we have found at least three reasons why creativity has its own chapter in this book:

1. Companies and organizations need innovation to develop and survive, which requires creativity in both leaders and employees.
2. Creativity creates meaning for individuals. Who doesn't want to feel alive at work, to contribute something important and maybe even achieve a state of "full-blast living"?
3. Creativity is something that can be practiced using mindfulness.

The tyranny of comparison and evaluation inhibits creativity

In light of this insight, it is surprising how often we put obstacles in the path to developing creativity. Let's start with some psychological inhibitors to creativity that we can immediately do something about: evaluation tyranny, fear of mistakes, the law of moderation, comparisons and the myth of talent.

• The tyranny of evaluation

This is perhaps the most inhibiting obstacle to personal expression. The most common reason we hesitate when given the opportunity to express ourselves creatively is the fear of other people's negative viewpoints. Positive reviews don't seem to be favorable from a creativity perspective either (remember the experiment mentioned in the introduction about the children painting). You need to remind yourself that all judgments are dependent on the context, and that no feedback is applicable to all situations. You can best withstand evaluation tyranny if you realize how uncreative it is to accept an individual evaluation without questioning it.

• Mistakes promote creativity
...while the fear of mistakes inhibits it. If you pay attention to your mistakes, they help you to explore new ways to act. Mistakes are context-based, like reviews. In one context, a mistake can be an error, while in another context it can be a surprising asset. For instance, when the American poet Robert Frost felt his poems did not measure up, he called them "exercises."

• Law of moderation
We tend to create laws and rules and when we use them we let ourselves become limited by them without questioning them. By reviewing the origin of the law using mindfulness and asking questions like, "Who made the rules?," "When and under what circumstances do they apply?," you are moving away from being rule-abiding to being guided by the rules.

• Comparison
We seem to be experts on frequently and unconsciously comparing ourselves to those we assess as incredibly creative. Therefore, we often fall short. Although comparison is a natural human tendency, you should remember that most social comparison will lead to future unhappiness, because there will always be people who are better than you are in any aspect. However, Ellen J. Langer reminds us that you can take advantage of other people's "greatness" if you remember the contextual influences that have contributed to their creative success. If you forget it, you will easily slip into another creativity-inhibiting effect, namely:

• The myth of talent
We tend to focus on the end result of the efforts of others when we compare ourselves to them. We call it talent, while ignoring the insecure beginning with struggles, uncertainty and a learning process through many years of training that the "creatively successful" have undergone. In this way, our perception of this widens the gap between our own talents and those of

others. In fact, probably, the real difference between those we perceive as talented and ourselves, is their willingness and ability to go forward into uncertainty despite the doubts, setbacks and failures.

Think about Zlatan Ibrahimovic! He would in all likelihood not have scored goal after goal with amazing creativity if he had not spent thousands of hours practicing, or allowed himself to be stopped by the obstacles and difficulties that he encountered along the way. It is possible that he may have been born with a unique gene for football, but this has not been established.

This leads us into the field of learning and expertize, which together with mindfulness, form the prerequisites for creativity being developed and channeled into innovation that can change society.

EXPERTIZE, DISCIPLINE AND SPONTANEITY

The IT company Google has been ranked as one of the most innovative companies in the world for several years. This is not only because employees have one free day a week to develop their ideas, or that they practice mindfulness. The wealth of innovation also rests fundamentally on the expertize of its IT technicians, developers and programmers. This successful combination of expertize, time and mindfulness training has also resulted in innovations such as Gmail and Google maps, as well as the mindfulness program "*Search Inside Yourself*".

An essential aspect of creativity is that it needs to be spontaneous. If our thoughts and behavior follow certain patterns, or are consciously considered and selected, they are by definition not creative. Meanwhile, it is easy to fall into the misconception that creativity and spontaneity would be the opposite of diligent training and discipline. Sometimes there seems to be the idea that training and expertize hamper spontaneous creativity.

Science journalist Karin Bojs commented on this at the Nobel Prize ceremony in 2010. She had interviewed physicist Andre Geim, who developed graphene-based nanomaterials. Geim talked a lot about intuition, and how he could tackle physics problems in an intuitive and almost emotional way. The whole point was that Andre Geim developed this ability only after having gone through a long and extraordinarily demanding training.

Karin Bojs says that this may be disappointing to those who think it is enough to be "creative" without the foundation of rigorous training.

Professor Jay Garfield illustrates this apparent contrast between purposeful, disciplined training and creative spontaneity in an interesting way. Garfield believes that through targeted effort, based on mindfulness, we can train ourselves to be kind, thoughtful and ethical. If we have the idea that we want to be good colleagues, friends or parents, we need not be satisfied with how things are presently. We can actually develop the qualities we value through purposeful training. In the beginning, we may need ethical rules to relate to, but the more we practice, the more natural these approaches become.

Garfield describes an interview the journalist Terry Gross made with jazz pianist Hank Jones. He asked Jones how improvisation works, and whether he knows which note is coming next. The journalist expected Jones to reply that when he is in the right mood, the notes emanate from him by themselves, without thought or intention. Instead, Jones replied, "Terry, what do you think all those years of intense training were for? I may not consciously control my fingers in the moment, but I'm concentrating a lot on the next two beats." Great jazz may be spontaneous, emphasizes Jones, but it is definitely not random. Improvisation also requires sensitivity to the other musicians in the group—a sensitivity that in itself must be spontaneous and not strained. It is, however, the product of countless hours of hard work.

Mindfulness, says Garfield, is deliberate, metacognitive attention that enables training, but the goal of this exercise is to let go in favor of spontaneous, creative perception and spontaneous action. We don't train to become automatic, "mindless" robots, but to be more spontaneously conscious and present in a deeper sense, pay attention to ourselves and others so that we can live life with the same effortless virtuosity as a skilled jazz musician who improvises a masterpiece.

Innovation requires not only the creative flow of ideas, but also knowledge—but not just any knowledge.

The book, *Presence*, by Peter M. Senge and his colleagues, puts forward the hypothesis that there are two main ways of learning that either inhibit or promote our creativity: the deductive and inductive.

The authors believe that our Western educational system, which still dominates the world, is based on a deductive learning tradition. It originates from industrialism and logic that is based on engineering, which assumes control, predictability and standardization. There is also the idea that the whole is composed of many parts, like the chassis of a car. According to this logic, the parts should sit in the right place and function effectively for the whole thing to work. If a part breaks, it needs to be repaired or replaced.

It is a logical way of thinking about machines, but not particularly applicable to a living system, such as a humans, a tree or an organization. The authors suggest that living systems grow, learn and change continually, according to their way of life. This learning, growth and change is, therefore, based, not on a dichotomy between the parts and the whole, but rather on an understanding of how the thinking and actions of each individual are related to and affects the whole.

Deductive learning involves assimilating knowledge that more or less confirms our earlier understanding. We are looking for facts and thought processes that we already recognize, and know that they are applicable. This is a way to increase our knowledge base. This reactive approach tends to make us rigid and defensive, regardless of the results. We stick to our familiar positions because we like to stay in our comfort zone and like to be "right." Deductive learning thereby inhibits new, unexpected and creative ways of thinking—and ultimately hampers innovation as well.

The second mode is inductive learning, which characterizes innovators.

When 150 leading scientists and leaders in a wide range of innovative activities were interviewed in *Presence*, it is precisely the transition from deductive to inductive learning that unites them. All have abandoned their habitual thinking and instead have acquired a greater understanding of how their own thinking and behavior is associated with and affects the world as a whole.

In other words, each outer innovation began with an inner personal change. W. Brian Arthur, an economist, puts it like this, "Every profound innovation is based on a single personal journey, seeking a deeper place from which this knowledge can reach the surface." This inner journey, says Arthur, is the basis of all creativity and innovation, whether it is in the field of science, the arts or in business. In summary, the authors say that this is also why innovative people often live in the paradoxical state of great confidence and profound humility. They know that their personal choices and actions make a difference, but often without knowing in advance how this will occur.

THE LINK BETWEEN CREATIVITY AND MINDFULNESS

The connection between mindfulness and creativity can be seen in that mindfulness contains a series of approaches, which forms the core or prerequisite for developing creativity.

Eleanor Rosch talks about mindfulness in the "early" part of the creative process. What she means by this is that all creativity begins in a conscious and alert mind. Unconditionally and without judgment, you open yourself to the situation and the problems within. Take, for example, a business where she worked.

"The manager's attitude to the employees was that they were a bunch of stubborn sheep that she tried in vain to push in the one direction. When she began doing the mindfulness exercise of "loving kindness", she began to see the individual employees and understand why they wouldn't do as she wanted. Only when the manager had found affinity for their differing abilities, was she able to start putting together creative teams with tasks that were a better fit for the preferences and desires of each employee. In order to get there, first she had to let go of the idea that she was in control of everything.

Let us give some more examples of how mindfulness and creativity are interrelated:

Beginner's mind

To connect to the "beginner's mind" means you experience the world attentively with fresh eyes and not through the grid of old experiences. It enables you to see the similarities between things you normally think are different, and differences between things you usually see as the same. This conscious view can arouse new reflections, thoughts and ideas. The opposite of this is to live through habitual repetition and turn on your autopilot, which has rigid and fixed patterns of action.

Christopher Engman, the CEO of an IT company in Stockholm, says after the whole company completed the CBMT mindfulness program that concept of beginner's mind is what changed him and his colleagues the most. It has permeated the entire company, and has facilitated a creative atmosphere at work.

"To never consider oneself fully trained. To listen carefully, even if someone is talking about something you already know, so you can learn something new. I could catch myself standing and talking to someone and automatically thinking: "I know that already," then I have tuned out and missed an opportunity... or if I sit in a meeting and think I have heard this before. Now, I tell myself to still listen, because I know that there will be something that I have not heard before. I think many in the company were influenced by this—to go into new situations with the attitude of a child, to be curious in a positive way and not to think that you know it all."

Disconnecting your autopilot

One aspect of relating creatively is that you see things as they really are, and not as they usually appear. There is a big risk that you will become blinkered when you are too confident that you are right and know how things are. Plenty of research supports this hypothesis, for example when interviewing witnesses who were confident of what they had seen, but who later turned out to be wrong—in other words, their overconfidence was not borne out in reality.

The alternative is being in full contact with your authentic experience and having the courage to believe in it. It may mean that you focus your attention on some aspect of your experience, or that you choose open attention. The creative process requires you to switch between these two perspectives.

Trust in your ability and intuition

You can rarely be sure of the results of what you do, so the world is uncontrollable to a large extent (at least, in the long term). This uncertainty underlies everything you do, whether you admit it or not. It doesn't make any difference whether it is about new or old ways of doing something, but facing the discomfort of ultimately not being in control of where your actions lead you is challenging. To then begin to think and do something new results in even more uncertainty and perhaps even more discomfort.

Making decisions shaped by mindfulness is about daring to choose the unknown or "new" you believe in—despite the discomfort and uncertainty.

Listen to the inner voice

Bill George, professor at Harvard Business School, talks about the little inner voice which is often being drowned out by our thoughts, feelings, constant doing and concerns about the past or future. George says that this little inner voice, or intuition as he calls it, has helped him make the right choices many times in his life.

On his website, he writes, "At one point in my career I had the opportunity to lead a business worth $500 million or to lead a business worth $100 million. The obvious rational choice would have been the first option, but my inner voice, the really excited feeling I had in my body, meant that I chose the second. The choice, based on intuition led to much learning, growth and future promotions. Intuition is often something that you can feel in your body, if we take the time to listen to it."

Attention promotes new thinking

Research shows that mindfulness training, both with open and directed attention, lays the foundation for a creative approach. One study showed that open attention involves a state that promotes divergent thinking, i.e. thinking that allows many new ideas. In addition, it seems that training in directed attention doesn't support convergent thinking, i.e. the idea that there is only one possible solution to one particular problem.

Another study of mindfulness and creativity showed how mindfulness training decreased cognitive rigidity, or strictly rule-based thinking. In the experiment, mindfulness practitioners had to solve six tasks. The first three tasks required complex solutions, while the rest were easier. The control group, which consisted of people who did not practice mindfulness, became more quickly frustrated than the mindfulness practitioners, who also found easier ways to solve the tasks. The authors concluded that the mindfulness practitioners hadn't been "blinkered" by experience, but had found more innovative and adaptive ways to act when faced with new challenges.

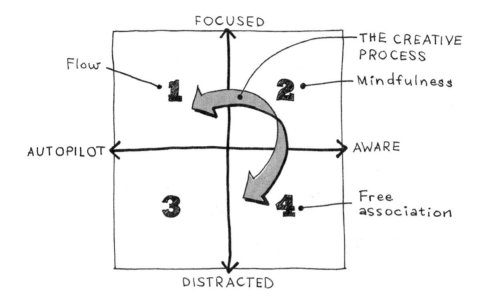

THE CREATIVE PROCESS

As mentioned earlier, creativity is a process whose various parts require different approaches. Let us now go back to the matrix of directed and open attention (chapter 4) and see how it is connected to the creative process:

In this figure, we have illustrated the creative process as it is formulated in five steps, according to Eleanor Rosch:

1. Preparation is where you become immersed, consciously or not, in a problem area that arouses your interest and curiosity (here, you can move between three of the quadrants: flow, mindfulness and free association).
2. Incubation time is when ideas roll around in a more unconscious way, without interference from your conscious, linear and logical thinking. During this time, unusual (creative) coincidences of thoughts and ideas

take place, sometimes in the early hours of the morning, in the state between sleep and wakefulness (free association).

3. Insight is the "Aha" or "Eureka!" moment. You realize how the pieces fit together. In real life, these insights come back several times and are safe-guarded by periods of incubation, evaluation and further development.

4. Evaluation is where you have to decide if the insight is valuable enough to be worth pursuing. This is often the most emotionally stressful phase, in which your own insecurities and questioning by others can determine the outcome. Is the idea really interesting, new, and valuable? It is a period of assessment (with mindfulness).

5. Further development is the phase that requires most of the hard work. Edison argued that creativity consists of 1 per cent inspiration and 99 per cent perspiration (or translated into the matrix: 1 per cent flow/free association and 99 per cent mindfulness).

These phases are not necessarily linear, but tend to overlap with each other or recur several times. No matter how each individual case appears, the model can facilitate your understanding of the challenges surrounding the creative process and what it takes to get through it.

Curiosity as a problem-solving skill

Consider for a moment where you usually get your best ideas. Is it at the computer, at the café, on the running track or in the lift?

Curiosity means that you are present with your whole experience (as opposed to when you solve problems based on rational reasoning). If you get into contact with this curiosity, you will notice how problems you have pondered will dissolve of their own accord. When you identify when and where you usually feel the most present and creative. Go there.

Tip from 91 creative people

(as conveyed by Mihaly Csikszentmihalyi):
- Try to be amazed/surprised by something every day.
- Try to surprise at least one person every day.
- Write down what has surprised you and how you have surprised others each day.
- Wake up in the morning with a specific goal to look forward to.
- When something raises a spark of interest, follow it.
- When you do something well, it will be enjoyable.
- Create time for reflection and rest.
- Find out what you like and what you dislike in life. Do more of what you like and less of what you dislike.
- Find a way to express that which moves you.
- See a problem from as many different angles as possible.
- Have as many different ideas as possible.
- Try to produce unlikely ideas.

The emotional impact you have as a leader can permeate an entire organization and, therefore, it is so important that you as a leader can control your emotions and not react to them.

Michael Chaskalson

CHAPTER 9

THE BIRCH TREE THAT CHANGED THE LIFE OF A CEO

HOW THE CHALLENGES OF A LEADER CAN BE OVERCOME BY MINDFULNESS

It has been said that man is a rational animal. All my life, I have been searching for evidence to support this.
Bertrand Russell

IT WAS STILL LIGHT, one evening early in May, and Peter was sitting in the car on his way home. The worst of the peak-hour traffic had subsided, since he usually worked overtime, although Peter seldom thought of it like that. He was a manager and managers work a lot. That's just how it is. And, if he wasn't at work, he was thinking about work. His wife, Anna, took care of most things at home to do with the children and the house. It was the division they had agreed upon and that was how it had continued.

The division of labor had functioned alright for many years, but recently Peter had felt that something was not quite right. He had become increasingly forgetful, restless and irritable. He found himself getting caught up in thoughts that often made him feel lonely, even though he was surrounded by his family or colleagues.

The spring evening was bathed in sunshine when Peter was on his way home, and thousands of trees had started to bud. Small delicate, light green shoots had unfurled and formed a soft carpet over the city. Some people were slowing down their pace to turn their gaze upwards. Others hurried past the cigarette butts, dirt and dog droppings that remained after the last piles of snow had melted. In the suburb where Peter lived, the change of the season was unmistakable. Both the oak and the birch trees in Peter's garden had started to bud. Blackbirds sang together, and a newly awakened lemon butterfly fluttered around.

When Peter turned off the engine in the driveway, he grabbed his jacket and briefcase as usual to rush into the house. However, when he got out of the car, he paused. Something felt different. Was it something about the color or the scent? He stood there transfixed, holding his mobile phone. He slowly studied the cobbled lane, the whitewashed building façade and the unkempt garden. This was his home, and the family house. He had lived here for more than 15 years, but now when he stood here and looked around, it appeared unusual, and strange. Had he ever stopped right here and looked at his house? He fought the impulse to run inside. There was something about the crisp spring air that tickled his nose. He took a deep breath of fresh air and let his gaze sweep over the garden. He almost fell over. There was a birch tree in the middle of the garden, just a few meters from his feet! It was an elongated narrow tree with small delicate green leaves at the tips of the branches. Peter blinked and looked again—yes, it was true. He had never noticed that tree before. How on earth did it get there?

Peter has another name, and has no wife or children. But, he does exist, and he was a successful CEO who had lived in the same house for over 15 years. There was a birch tree in his garden that he walked past every day, without noticing. He did this at least twice a day from Monday to Sunday for 15 years—that is 10,920 times—without seeing it.

Just like Peter, this man discovered his own birch tree one day after following suggestions given to him in a mindfulness course for leaders. It was a discovery that really changed his life. It changed his attitude towards himself and his abilities, how he related to his environment and to other people and, most importantly, it changed his leadership.

Jeremy Hunter, Professor of Psychology, related this incident during a mindfulness conference in Dalarna, Sweden. Jeremy Hunter has been running mindfulness leadership courses at one of the most prestigious business schools in the world for more than ten years. It was during one of these courses that he gave the man in the story the task of using his beginner's mind to describe a daily activity. He says that the story of the birch tree is an example of how automated habitual behavior prevents us from experiencing reality as it is, which can be directly detrimental to a leader. It is perhaps not so much about not seeing a tree in his own garden, but as Hunter reasons, "Now if the man did not see the tree that he passed every day, could there be other parts of reality that he walked past without noticing—people at work, other people's thoughts and perspectives on various issues, warning signs, innovative solutions? If we broaden our perspective, would the collapse of Lehman Brothers and the Wall Street crash in 2008 have taken place if the elite economic leaders had really seen what was happening, while it was happening? The fact is that everything is interdependent. How can you lead others unless you can lead yourself?"

Jeremy Hunter has led mindfulness courses for leaders since the late 1990s. When he talks about his experiences and how he thinks, he happily draws connections between a butterfly flapping its wings and tsunamis, in other words, between small and large events. According to him, what each individual leader thinks and does in each moment has consequences, not only on the individual and the organizational level, but it also contributes to the whole of society. The man with the birch tree was one of Hunter's many participants who used this insight to begin making changes in his leadership. He began to actively observe his surroundings, listen to his employees and realize that he didn't see everything and didn't know everything.

The difficulty in perceiving reality as it actually is, says Hunter, is one of the big challenges for leaders. Another is finding a balance between different objectives and values. Bill George, a professor at Harvard Business School, believes that all leaders are grappling to navigate successfully between the personal inner values you really want to promote and the ever-increasing external pressure to deliver short-term economic results. Bill George is also convinced that it is possible to balance professional success with personal success, which is more important, but also more difficult to measure. This conviction is based on the observation that, at the beginning of one's career, very few people, if any, act dishonestly or harm others intentionally, which, of course, is often the consequence of leadership characterized by maximizing short-term profit.

Bill George's hypothesis has been confirmed in a study by his colleague Clayton Christensen, also a professor at Harvard Business School. Christensen says that even former NASDAQ chairman Bernie Madoff (sentenced in 2009 to 150 years in prison for embezzling billions) and Enron's Jeff Skilling (sentenced to 26 years for embezzling employee retirement money, among other things) probably intended to live honest lives at the beginning of their careers. What happened was that they started to make exceptions to the rule, with the excuse of "just this once," as if a small slip didn't count. Then, the exception was made again and again.

If Madoff and Skilling had joined Bill George and Jeremy Hunter's courses, it is possible that these exceptions may never have happened, because a leader dedicated to mindfulness knows that every action has a long-term impact. Bill George has taken up this idea. In his course, Authentic Leadership Development (ALD), which has become one of the most sought-after courses at Harvard University, George teaches tomorrow's leaders to measure success in another way, rather than in terms of monetary wealth or achieving a particular position. He wants to see success measured by the contribution to positive change in the lives of their colleagues, in the organization of their own family and in society, as a whole. By rooting leadership in conscious values, George believes that the students (and even the experienced leader who runs the course) will be better equipped to meet these requirements, rather than only working for short-term economic goals.

The core of this education is training in mindfulness, which means that you can both observe and participate in every moment you are in, while being mindful of the long-term impact of your actions. This prevents you from stumbling onto a path that will lead you away from your values.

Michael Chaskalson, a pioneer in mindfulness training for leaders in the UK, believes that the increased interest in mindfulness for leaders is related to the financial crises in recent years. "Before this happened, development in the West seemed to go swimmingly. All the leaders seemed to believe that they had the answer to what they should do. However, now the old maps are no longer true, and most leaders have some uncertainty about what to do. This has resulted in an increasing interest in exploring new ways of dealing with life."

Jeremy Hunter and Michael Chaskalson describe how mindfulness can contribute to one of these new ways in their book, Making The Mindful Leader. Based on their own experiences and research in the field, they affirm that many leaders have difficulty discerning what kind of problems they face: if it is a simple, known technical problem that can be solved with existing skills, or a complex problem that requires adaptive solutions. According to the authors, a common mistake that managers make is to identify adaptive problems as technical, with the result that they are using yesterday's solutions for today's problems. This is a result of the human tendency to unconsciously react with a fixed pattern of action and habitual ways of attributing meaning.

What mindfulness can contribute is to loosen up this habit. Leaders need to evolve towards a more sophisticated way of understanding, thinking, acting and relating because an increasing number of problems are adaptive in nature.There are also different degrees of complexity that need to be understood. Sometimes the problem is well-known (such as the water supply in a desert town being limited), but the solution is uncertain (shall we transport water from another water hole, invest in water treatment and recycling or are there other ways?). Sometimes the reality is so complex that both the problem and the solution are unknown, such as the global environmental issue. For this issue, the problems cannot even be precisely specified and, therefore, neither the problem nor the solution can be formulated using accepted "truths." Jeremy Hunter says, "I believe that leaders, who live in harmony with their environment and their contemporaries, understand and feel that something is not quite functioning as it should, but we don't always know what is not working or what the solution looks like. At the same time, you are responsible for making decisions and guiding institutions that affect many other people. This inner experience of having overall responsibility is very onerous. There is great pressure to deliver results, but the updated navigation maps are missing.

Missing map updates is certainly not a new problem. Professor and management consultant Peter Drucker pointed out the value of direct experience, already in the mid-1900s. In the 1970s, Drucker spent two years at the car company General Motors (GM) to gain a deep understanding of the production and decision-making process. What he discovered was an overvaluation of the automated analytical approach and an underestimation of direct experience. Over many years of economic stability, producing American cars that were relatively low in quality had been successful, but when management ignored the fact that cheaper and better cars began to be imported from Japan, it went downhill.

According to Drucker, this inability to rely on direct experience was the reason why the car imperium ended up in the backwaters for many years. With his experience, Drucker adapted Descartes famous words, "I think, therefore I am" to "I experience, therefore I am."

What the management at GM did (or any other leader who has not adapted the organization to new conditions) was not very surprising from a psychological point of view. Research shows that habitual, unconscious thinking, feeling and acting is as high as 90 per cent (!) of all human behavior, according to some studies. As well as this, what we know about these automated action patterns is that when they are triggered, it happens the same way every time—mechanically and without regard to changes in circumstances. Therefore, they can possibly work well in times of stability, which was true for many years at GM, but when changes take place, which occurs periodically, there is a high risk that the old recipe for success no longer corresponds to the new circumstances.

What can be done?

The first thing a leader needs to do in order to move from automatic to conscious behavior, is to practice focusing his/her attention. It is only when you can hold your attention for long enough, that you have the opportunity to consider the choices, solve complex problems and achieve the results you consider to be the most favorable.

Jeremy Hunter says that most of the leaders who seek out his mindfulness courses are in a divided state of stress, inadequacy and confusion. In other words, their ability to direct their attention is often completely out of action.

IT development has probably also contributed to this fragmentation. The long-term psychological consequences of text and email beeps and chat windows is as yet unknown, but when they are used without restriction, we know that it divides our attention. Jeremy Hunter compares it to the introduction of the car.

"When the first cars hit the market, there were no traffic rules and no laws at all. It soon became chaos on the roads. I think we are at a similar stage. We have introduced all these amazing devices, but we have no consensus on the best way to relate to them. The approach varies in different organizations. In some companies, employees are forced to have their chat windows open all the time, because it is necessary to be available constantly. What might not have been thought through, is that automatic interruption affects the quality of the attention and thus the overall performance of the employees. This gives leaders quite a challenge to identify what the organization really wants to achieve."

HOW MINDFULNESS AFFECTS LEADERSHIP

The example of the man with the birch tree was an illustration of how autopilot and the lack of directed attention prevents us from seeing reality as it is. However, it also shows that a divided or automated mind can be repaired. As well as this, mindfulness in a leader is no different to mindfulness in anyone else. The training is the same and it begins as a slow restoration of the attention function in the brain.

Research shows us that directed and open attention fires up our performance. We know that it increases a sense of connection between people and it makes us feel like part of a larger entity, organization or the world. If you find yourself in a management position where you need to get things done and relate constructively to other people, then attention is a basic ability that you will need, just as we need to be able to read and write in order to become employable.

Using our attention to regulate our emotions is something that Michael Chaskalson works with a lot with in his mindfulness courses. His experience is that leaders need to get a better understanding of how contagious their own emotional state is, and how this affects the relationships we are attempting to build with others.

"The emotional impact you have as a leader can permeate an entire organization and, therefore, it is so important for you to control your emotions and not to react to them. Imagine a leader of a workgroup facing a deadline, with a major task to be delivered, no matter what. The clock is ticking and there is no time to waste. Imagine then that a new junior recruit comes along with a naive proposal and the manager rudely waves him away saying, "No, what a bad idea!" What do you think happens to the recruit, how will he react? What will his contribution to the organization be after this event? Will he even be able to contribute to the final stage, or get the job done? Will he dare to come up with a new proposal for the rest of the week, or in the weeks ahead, or at all?"

When Michael Chaskalson described this scenario during a lecture, an elderly man came up to him afterwards. The man had a high position at a large company and said that during the lecture, it dawned on him that he had been that sort of manager, who had waved people away and bellowed at his employees. He had not realized how his behavior affected the people around him. It had certainly not been his intention. He had only done what he thought was right. Not until now, when most of his professional life was behind him, and when he gave himself time to reflect, did he understand how his emotional reactions had affected others. "I think it was very brave of him to reveal himself like that, Michael Chaskalson noted, because it was a heavy realization that had struck the man."

Effective relations affect not only the work environment, but also the results. As already mentioned, adaptive problem solving often requires complex coordination between multiple parts of the brain, which presupposes that the relationship is characterized by a more informal and open-minded point of view. It has been shown that when the leader is emotionally attached to his/her employees, he/she can also persuade and motivate them to act in a way that might be uncomfortable or go against the employees' own short-term interests. It has been well established that the leader's behavior and attitudes affect employees' attitudes, behavior and well-being, and now more and more results are showing that leaders who have been practicing mindfulness contribute to better performance and the greater well-being of their employees.

In the book Mindful Leadership, a number of writers, organizational consultants and mindfulness instructors have compiled the latest research and their own personal experience of what mindfulness training for leaders can achieve. Some of their conclusions about leaders who practice mindfulness are that they:

- Can control their temper and handle emotional reactions better.
- Find it easier to discern between a technical and adaptive problem by shifting from conceptual to perceptual vision, i.e. they are able to perceive the situation as it actually is and not on the basis of a rigid model based on past experience. These abilities of objectivity and clear-sightedness also lead to better decisions.
- Have increased their attention span and improved their working memory.
- Have developed higher levels of empathy.
- Have achieved greater innovation.
- Experience greater control and inner strength and feel confident that they can handle the situations that arise.
- See choices that they previously couldn't see.

Take a break before you need it!

When should we as leaders do mindfulness training? Common reasons for leaders to attend a course are that:

- They are lost.
- They are stuck in a re-organization and don't know how to navigate their way through.
- They are not satisfied with the role they have and are looking for a new one.
- They feel that their job no longer provides enough meaning.
- They feel overwhelmed by everything that needs to be done.
- They don't get enough done.
- They may be stuck in distracting habits, such as often becoming angry.
- They stress too much.
- They put their energy into the wrong things.
- They have been rejected by their partners or at work.
- They are tired.
- They are sick.

This has often been going on for an unnecessarily long time. When Jeremy Hunter interviewed 30 leaders who practiced mindfulness, including their reasons for starting training, one third of participants had been diagnosed with life-threatening illnesses. He concludes from this that it often takes something very drastic in life before seeking change. He notes, "People are in pretty bad shape when they start. 'Take a break before you need one!' is a good motto. Unfortunately, people don't do this often enough."

Even though it provides greater benefits if the entire workplace undergoes mindfulness training, as Michael Chaskalson sees it, there is nothing to prevent individual leaders from beginning training.

"Some of the leaders I have worked with relate too passively to their organizations, and don't see the opportunity they have to change things. I have worked with leaders of a major financial institution who told me that I could not imagine how difficult it would be for them to go back to work with new skills. The influence of the prevailing culture was too dominant. My answer was "Change it then! You are the leader, otherwise you should leave the organization. You must have bolder leadership. If you as a leader cannot change anything, who will do it?"

Research shows ...

An independent evaluation of the CBMT (Corporate-Based Mindfulness Training) program was made in 2012 after a big leadership team from the insurance company, If, in Denmark had undergone an eight-week course. During the course, participants focused on mindfulness, which was defined as:

1. Focused (directed) attention.
2. To do one thing at a time and to be able to shift attention when you want.
3. Inner awareness.
4. To be aware of what is going on internally: thoughts, emotions and the state of your mind and body.
5. External awareness.
6. Being aware of the surrounding conditions and how our presence and what we are doing is affecting others.

7. Disengaging the autopilot and habitual behaviors.
8. Driving somewhere without remembering how you got there and sometimes not even knowing why you went there.

Jochen Reb, Professor at the Singapore Management University and the University of Cambridge, who conducted the study, saw a significant improvement in all four aspects. The greatest difference was with focused attention, which increased significantly. Other results of the program were that:

• Job satisfaction increased.
• The emotional commitment to work increased.
• Emotional exhaustion decreased.
• OCB (organizational citizenship behavior) increased, which involves better performance, beyond the scope of the allocated tasks.

They also measured how the amount of time participants spent on the training affected the results. Ten minutes had a result, but the more they practiced, the greater the job satisfaction. It also correlated with fewer participants considering changing jobs, after having done the course.

These results have been confirmed in other studies.

Wait attentively

Use "waiting" as part of your attention training. When you are waiting for your luggage, or when you are travelling by plane, taxi or public transport, focus on your breathing, then the training won't take up any more of your time.

Use meetings for awareness training. Turn off the computer and mobile phone, and really try to listen to what others are saying, without thinking that you need to determine whether it is good or bad, right or wrong. Listen to the words and the undertones, and see if there's anything you haven't heard before. Ask questions if you don't understand.

Train your beginner's mind

Imagine that you are seeing your workplace as if you saw it for the very first time. What does it look like? What sounds can you hear? How does it smell? How does it feel? Which people are around you? Avoid thinking about things or people as beautiful or ugly, good or bad, just describe everything as it is.

Don't focus too much on problems

Many leaders see themselves as responsible for solving problems, with the best of intentions. When problems become a constant focus, they begin to lose the ability to see new solutions. Try to shift the focus from problems to finding strength in what works. What are our strengths? What is good in this situation? How can we learn from this? How can we grow, based on what actually works?

Talk IT

Have an on-going dialogue about how to handle IT. How does being continuously availability affect the quality of attention to other tasks? Should mobile phones remain on in a meeting, or stay in a box outside?

Develop your empathy

Train to create better relationships with your employees by developing empathy. Michael Chaskalson gives this advice in five steps:

1. Note the behavior of others.
This is not so much about reading body language, but involving the so-called mirror neurons. By being present and aware of another person's gestures, posture and actions, this activates mirror neurons in your brain. You might even be able to imitate a gesture, with sensitivity. How does it feel? What is your body telling you?

2. Zoom in on your own feelings and emotions.
Become aware of your breathing and feel it. Focus on your feelings, and bodily sensations. This conscious attention to your own experience stimulates the part of the brain that allows you to learn from the experiences of other people.

3. Pay attention to your employees' eyes and facial expressions.
Paul Ekman has demonstrated how emotions such as anger, fear, disgust, sadness and happiness, are expressed in our faces as clear signals that others can identify. These clues can sometimes take up micro-expressions that pass by in an instant and can change quickly. With directed attention, you will have a much better chance of and the ability to detect these changes.

4. Pay attention to your own thoughts and actively imagine what another person is thinking.
When you notice another person's behavior and facial expressions, you begin to get a sense of his/her feelings and sensations, partly by reading your own thoughts. Make a note of that and imagine the thoughts that the other person may be having. Since man has a natural aptitude for empathy, your thoughts will probably align themselves with the other person.

5. Check with others and keep yourself open!

Thoughts are not facts. Always check with the other person to make sure what you think they are thinking and feeling is really what they are thinking and feeling. Ask open-ended questions and be prepared to change your opinion.

Allow enough time

The vast majority of tasks a leader has to deal with require a considerable amount of uninterrupted time. Set aside large blocks of time in the calendar—at least 4 hours for complex problem solving. Devote yourself only to what you have planned to do during this time. Turn off the phone and use autoreply for your email.

Training mindfulness is like going to your own mental gym.

CHAPTER 10

CBMT – A MINDFULNESS TRAINING PROGRAM

TO ESTABLISH A HABIT

As we mentioned earlier, directed attention is a limited resource, and to carry out an action using self-control and willpower requires a lot of patience and energy. Once you've decided to develop the skill of mindfulness in practice, be prepared to give it time.

A research team at Community College London, led by Philippa Lally, found that it takes 60 days on average to establish a new habit leading to behavior promoting good health. This same principle applies to developing mindfulness training as a natural part of life. Change is no quick fix – it is slow but sure. If you are persistent, you will be rewarded with a conscious, healthy mind that is capable of living in the present moment.

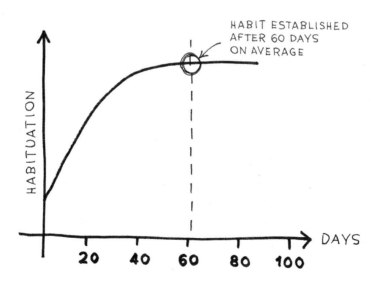

HABIT ESTABLISHED
AFTER 60 DAYS
ON AVERAGE

HABITUATION

DAYS

20   40   60   80   100

Train on your own

It is not easy to practice mindfulness on your own. The training itself is easy to understand and carry out. Despite the thousands of research studies, mindfulness is not "rocket science." Anyone with a functioning human brain has the ability to direct their attention and awareness to the present moment with focus and presence. The really hard part is getting down to action and actually doing it. The big challenge is to set aside time each day for training. The amount of time is up to you, but regular exercise is required in order to achieve the positive effects we've written about in this book.

Having access to an experienced instructor definitely facilitates training. Training with others is also helpful, especially in the workplace, where the established habits of corporate culture lead us in other directions. If you are the only one at work who is attempting to utilize attention, awareness and presence during the working day, it can feel lonely and tough. Therefore, we recommend that you enlist one or more colleagues, and preferably managers and HR personnel as well. If there is not already a committed mindfulness instructor within your organization, we recommend the CBMT (Corporate-Based Mindfulness Training) program outlined here. Training together, or individually with the support of each other, helps in the same way that a running group increases the joy and motivation to run.

We strongly recommend working with a qualified trainer to implement mindfulness training in your organization. If this does not seem like a viable option, we recommend that you find a mindfulness group outside of work. Practicing with others once a week or once a month makes it much easier to train on your own in between.

We have presented exercises advice and exercises on how to apply mindfulness, based on aspects that may be particularly relevant in previous chapters. In this chapter, we have collected general and basic mindfulness exercises designed especially for those who deal with information management and human relations at work. The exercises can be done alone, although it will have a greater effect if the whole group, department and, especially, the whole organization participates.

CBMT – A TRAINING PROGRAM FOR MINDFULNESS AT WORK

We hope that you are eager to get started with your training now. See below for an overview of a sample training program for mindfulness in the workplace. With a program length between 5 and 11 weeks, it has been specifically designed for companies and organizations, in order to support mindfulness training in a hectic working life. It has been developed by a team of researchers, mindfulness experts and leaders from the business community. The CBMT program is presently offered in 23 countries around the world, in both large and small companies such as Accenture, IKEA, Carlsberg, Sony, Google and MasterCard.

The CBMT program consists of three parts:

1. Formal mindfulness training – the ABCD exercise, described in Chapter 4
2. Work applications – areas of your job suitable for the application of mindfulness
3. Mental strategies – which make you more efficient, happier and less stressed (and will also change the atmosphere in your workplace).

These three tracks run in parallel. During a CBMT program, the participants have opportunities to share their challenges and discuss attitudes and themes in workshops every week.

1. Formal mindfulness training

Most people engage in some form of physical exercise, by going to the gym, walking, jogging or playing sport. The reason for this is that physical training leads to better fitness and gets us in better shape, which benefits us in many aspects of our daily life.

Mindfulness training is like going to our own mental gym. By spending ten minutes every day on the ABCD exercises training focused and open attention, you strengthen the ability of your mind to focus and be aware. In the same way as with improved physical fitness, you benefit from this improved mental fitness in your daily activities, both at work and in your free time.

The ABCD method, described in chapter 4, is the core mindfulness exercise in the CBMT program. At the beginning of the program, the emphasis is on training directed attention/focus. As the program progresses, you change the way you use the ABCD exercises, from directed attention to training in open attention. The instruction is changed so that you develop open and allowing awareness, which notices everything that arises in the mind, without judging or evaluating it. That which was previously treated as a distraction (e.g. experiences in the body, sounds in the room, thoughts, mental images, etc.) are now objects of your attention. The important thing is that you are constantly aware and present, but the focus of your attention is no longer limited and narrow—but open and wide.

How long?

Ten minutes of formal mindfulness training a day is sufficient—the most important thing is that you train regularly. The effects will be greater if you train for 20 or 45 minutes, but 10 minutes will have a strong positive effect.

Where?

The only thing you need is somewhere to sit, with all the phones switched off and the door closed. At many companies where CBMT is implemented, a conference room is often reserved for mindfulness training, typically for one session in the morning, and one in the afternoon.

When?

If you train on your own, we recommend formal training before going to work. For many people, the morning works best. They find that the environment is often quieter, which affects their training. It is also easier to add a new habit in connection with other normal routines, and morning is the time of day that is generally most controlled by routine.

If you train in a group at the workplace, training can occur at any convenient time, preferably when everyone is there. If you are geographically dispersed, or travel a lot, then training can be done individually. To support daily training, the CBMT exercises are available in the Potential Project smartphone app, with reminder functions, and a logbook.

2. Applied mindfulness: Work applications

Mindfulness is not intended as an additional chore, but rather as a change in attitude towards all kinds of activities. The aim is to develop focus, presence and awareness in all areas of work. In addition to the formal mindfulness training, it is important that you select key activities at work in order to tailor the training as much as possible to your needs.

Consider which areas of increased focus and awareness can be integrated in your daily work. Examples of these areas include managing email, prioritizing, goal focus, communication, creativity and innovation, as well as leadership related themes (such as how to manage change, and authentic leadership).

3. Mental strategies

With training, everyone has the potential to become more successful, cheerful and friendly, even in stressful situations and under pressure. Developing a beneficial mental attitude towards yourself and your surroundings is a way to realize this potential.

The CBMT program includes eight mental strategies that can be developed within an organizational context. By training awareness, patience, acceptance, kindness, joy, non-judgment, beginner's mind, and letting go, this increases your ability to regulate your emotions, improves social relationships and develops a greater degree of psychological flexibility.

Psychological flexibility means that you apply the approach that is most appropriate to each situation. Feel free to discuss these attitudes with your colleagues and managers in relation to your work situation. Experience shows that openness about attitude and work culture have a positive impact on the behavior of the individual and organization as a whole that is game-changing. The way you act serves as a model for others and the way you embrace these favorable policies affects your colleagues and your environment more than you might think.

CBMT PROGRAM, WEEK 1

Mindfulness training: Directed attention

Mental strategy # 1: Presence

We tend to let our mind wander back to the past and into the future. However, the fact is that the past is gone and the future has not yet arrived—the only thing that we ever experience is the present moment. All of life consists of "the present moment." When you mentally disappear off into the past or future, you are not present and do not experience the richness of your life.

Being present in the moment does not require you to change your life or what you are doing in a practical sense. It is simply a shift in your attention—a conscious decision to be present in every moment. It is this type of attention or awareness that you cultivate in mindfulness training—a constant relating to that which is right here, right now.

This is how to train your awareness in your daily mindfulness practice:

Be aware of each breath as you inhale. Be aware of each breath as you exhale. Be aware of each distraction—and let go of it, that's all. Be present with each breath, without involving yourself in thoughts of the previous breath and the next. Mindfulness training is not just ten minutes of awareness, but more specifically, it is the awareness of each breath for ten minutes.

Use this method in your daily sessions this week.

The past is gone and the future has not yet arrived.
The only thing that you really have is this moment.
Life consists of a long chain of moments. When your
mind wanders to the past or the future, you will lose
the precious experience of being in the present. Be fully
present in this moment, and the next moment and each
following moment

Where are you right now?

Theme # 1: Working with mindfulness

When you are working with mindfulness, you will be fully present and aware of what you are doing. The result is a clearer focus throughout the day, a feeling of having achieved more at the end of the day and much greater satisfaction and joy in everything you do. Working with mindfulness doesn't make you slower, just smarter.

Multitasking (having "several balls in the air" at the same time) may seem like a shortcut, but new research shows that multitasking makes you less effective. Multitasking impairs your view, creates stress, gives poor results, prevents creativity and creates bad habits. The brain gets tired of having to multitask for long periods, and as a result of that, it slows down during the day. Working with your full attention on one task at a time is a way to recharge your mental batteries.

The principles of working with mindfulness are:

- Stay focused on what you choose.
- Consciously select which distractions you want to get involved with.
- Be fully aware of what you are doing, and direct your attention to it.
    - When the phone rings, give the conversation your full attention—or call back when you can.
    - When you get email, read it and answer it with full attention—or let it wait.
    - When a colleague asks you for your time, give them your full attention—or say that you will get back to them.

Don't let distractions dominate your life. Consciously choose to focus on your work and your life without letting distractions (phone calls, text messages, emails, colleagues, noise) determine the focus for you. Manage distractions in the same way as in the ABCD training.

Use the same principles in your private life—focus your full attention on cooking, washing and being together with your family and friends.

CBMT PROGRAM, WEEK 2

Mindfulness training: Directed attention

Mental strategy # 2: Patience

When you practice mindfulness, you may get a thought that says, "What am I doing here? I could get something done instead!" This is when you need patience. Sit there as long as you had planned, and don't give in to the restlessness that tries to stop you.

Patience is also a good attitude when you experience something unpleasant, such as physical pain, stress, anger, or grief. Being patient in this context means that you have the courage to stay with whatever arises, without just following your first impulse to push something away or to escape. When you run away, it is very likely that the same obstacles will return later, sometimes in a disguised form. An unpleasant feeling can only be solved where it arises, so stay with it, meet it head on, and manage it by observing it neutrally. In this way, you can overcome it and make it easier to manage the next time.

> Patience is having the courage to face what is unpleasant—to stay with it and observe it without trying to change it. Don't follow your first impulse to escape when you feel restless, angry, bored, or sad. If you try to escape the feeling, it will return. Be brave and stay with the feeling, and it will dissolve.

> A problem can only be solved in the mind that experiences it.

Theme # 2: Mindful breaks

Mindful breaks is a simple technique that helps you restore your focus and energy throughout the day.

Your brain has two different ways to work: conceptual and perceptual. The conceptual state is about "doing" (doing mode). It is a state of mind in which the brain plans and thinks about everything you need to do. Most of us find ourselves in the conceptual state of most of our lives.

The perceptual state of mind is a state of "being" (being mode). This is a state of observing in mind which is free from thoughts and solutions. Usually, the conceptual mode is in top gear, which will help us achieve what we want to do. However, the brain's resources are limited, and it gets tired if we do not get a break now and then.

Taking breaks and consciously coming into contact with the perceptual state of "being" makes it possible for you to be attentive to your physiological state, and to gain information in the form of emotions and other signals. Having a rest using mindfulness helps you break the autopilot and get back to yourself, to regain control of your attention.

- The technique is simple: once an hour, let go of what you are doing at that moment and follow three breaths, using the ABCD method.
- How do you remind yourself? Although the technology is simple, the challenge is to remember to do the exercise. It may be helpful to download a mindfulness app with the reminder feature on your mobile.

CBMT PROGRAM, WEEK 3

Mindfulness training: Directed attention

Mental strategy # 3: Kindness

If you maintain a positive state of mind, there will be no room for negativity. Unfortunately, that is easier said than done. The mind does not always have the mental fitness required to select its focus and state of mind. Mindfulness training gives you the mental abilities necessary to maintain a positive state of mind. It helps you keep your words and actions in line with your goals and values.

The most positive state of mind is kindness, which is the neurological antidote to emotions such as jealousy, hatred and anger. Kindness doesn't just quiet negative tendencies, it pulls them up by the roots. There is no room for anger when you are kind. Kindness has been proven to have positive effects on our psychological as well as physical well-being. Anger, on the other hand, has been proven to have negative effects.

The first step towards kindness is to be kind to yourself. When you are kind to yourself, you will have the ability to be kind to others. When you are at peace with yourself, you can help others to experience the same. Can you think of a situation where you felt happy and at peace, yet initiated conflicts with other people?

When you practice mindfulness with kindness, you embrace yourself and all experiences with kindness. Whatever you are experiencing, let go of it. All your worries—embrace them with kindness.

Be kind to yourself—be caring and accepting. Give yourself the time and space you need, then you will be able to be truly kind to others.

Being kind to others is the greatest source of joy and happiness. The wisest form of self-interest is to be of help to others. A smile is the shortest distance between two people.

Theme # 3: Goal setting

If you don't know which port you are sailing towards, no wind is favorable.
Seneca

Setting clear goals for your personal and private life is the first step towards achieving them. Without clear objectives, there is nothing to aim for, and your actions will lack deeper purpose. No matter how efficient you are in all aspects of your life, you will not be moving in the right direction if you have not clearly defined your goals. Sometimes you will be caught up in the stress of daily life, and struggle to climb to the top of the ladder in front of you. However, what's the point of getting to the top of the ladder, if you discover that it was leaning against the wrong wall?

Are you aware of important goals in your life? Do you spend time, on a regular basis, considering if the ladder you are climbing is leaning against the right wall?

Imagine the last working day of your life. All your colleagues have gathered together to say goodbye and to wish you luck. Imagine that you can read their thoughts. What would you wish that they were thinking about you? How would you like to be remembered after your working life? Such a simple reflection can help you define the goals that are uniquely important to you. Go through the same process for your private life. How would you like to be remembered by your family and friends?

During the coming week, take regular breaks to define your most important goals.

CBMT PROGRAM, WEEK 4

Mindfulness training: Directed attention

Mental strategy # 4: Beginner's mind

No moment is quite like another. Everything is changing and everything is new. Seeing things as if for the first time, opens us to unlimited potential in ourselves, as well as in others, in all situations. This is a great contrast to our usual way of looking at things, which is conditioned by our old habitual perception.

When you meet someone you know well, you can ask yourself if you see the person as he or she really is, or if you only see a reflection of what you already know about the person. Do you see the clear, present reality, or a collection of old memories?

It is easy to develop beginner's mind with mindfulness training. Try to discipline yourself to stay with something unpleasant that occurs during a session, such as the feeling of itching somewhere on the body. If you let yourself sit with the feeling, without reacting to it, first of all you will notice that it reduces by itself after a while (just like some things seem to disappear—because everything changes).

Afterwards, you will realize that you probably exaggerated the experience of itching. While it was occupying your attention, it appeared to be the largest and most important thing in your life. When it went away, from a more realistic perspective, you could see that it had just been a feeling of an itch. The simple truth is that tiny electrical signals were communicated between the point where it itched and your brain. This in itself has no intrinsic properties such as good or bad, pain or pleasure, right or wrong. If any of this was present in your experience, it was added as part of your habitual way of experiencing the situation.

With mindfulness training, you will discover that you can have the same experience of relating to strong physical pain, difficult emotions and persistent thoughts that you had with the itch. Being with these experiences helps you to see things from a more realistic and relative perspective, both during mindfulness training and in life in general. You will get access to a perspective through which the difficult aspects of life become less difficult, not because they change, but because you change how you relate to them.

> Everything changes, but your mind doesn't always follow suit. Do you see people in front of you as they really are? Do you see the thing or situation as it is, or do you see a reflection of what you are used to seeing?
> Note everything with curiosity, as if for the first time. When you see everything as it is, you open your mind to finding the positive potential in everything.

Theme # 4: Clear priorities

We often get carried away during our busy days at work. We tend to do what we have in front of us right now, and follow the activities that are written in the calendar. However, take a moment to consider the difference between being active and being productive. You are likely to find that just because you are active, it doesn't necessarily mean that you are being productive. Writing lots of emails can be active, but perhaps not very productive.

According to the Pareto principle described in chapter 6, often 80 per cent of your effort at work is taken up by activities that only give you 20 per cent of your results. Conversely, you reap 80 per cent of your results from 20 per cent of your effort. Therefore the essence of productivity must be to prioritize the activities that deliver the best results. To determine what these are, you must constantly reconcile your activities with your main goal.

You can use the gears of a car as an analogy to choosing the correct priority. If you drive 50 kph in first gear, the engine will be very active and noisy, but it will also use a lot of petrol and overheat. However, if you drive 50 kph in fifth gear, you will have a quiet, steady engine which uses little fuel and can continue to drive for hours. The only difference is which gear you choose. It is the same at work—by choosing the right priorities, you can get very far in a short time, without feeling overworked, and you will be able to continue for a long time.

Instead of prioritizing what is in your calendar, schedule your priorities. An easy way to ensure that you spend time on the right tasks is to take a few minutes to decide which of these are your main priorities. These tasks will bring you closer to your goals. Then take five minutes every morning to write down the priorities that will take you further along with the least effort. Do the same thing for fifteen minutes on a weekly basis, by writing down all the priorities for the week. Then do the same thing every month.

CBMT PROGRAM, WEEK 5

Mindfulness training: Open attention

Mental strategy # 5: Joy

Your entire nervous system responds strongly to your mental state. How you feel has a big impact on your body and performance. To strengthen the positive state of mind is an effective way to get better at what you are already good at. To a large extent, this is about how you manage your attention and focus. It is not possible to switch off negative thoughts, but you can choose to direct your attention to something that is constructive.

For example, you can consciously take note of everything you have that gives you joy in your life. When you rejoice in something, your resources increase, both physically and mentally. You will be better at solving problems and you will learn more quickly. Your social skills will increase and allow you to develop new contacts and consolidate those that you have already made. Your physical resources will strengthen and facilitate better health. From a psychological perspective, you will develop greater resilience and optimism.

Develop joy through mindfulness training. Do this by letting yourself enjoy the training. Relax while you sit for ten minutes. You don't need to do anything. You don't need to be the best.

Your life is filled with things you want to do well—to care for your family, friends and career. Mindfulness is not just another task. Mindfulness is your time and your life. Mindfulness is those minutes every day that you really give to yourself, so make sure that you take advantage of them.

Theme # 5: Clear planning

The bad news: time flies.
The good news: you're the pilot.
Michael Altshuler

As we all know, we never find time for anything. If we want to have time, we need to take time. If you have clear priorities for what needs to be done, you must take the time to plan your time. You need to take regular breaks to plan and schedule the highest priority.

It is essential for you to plan your time, so that you can make time for the priorities you need to do in order to achieve your goals. Planning your time consciously is also a crucial habit to create the conditions that make it possible to maintain focus and awareness in the second quadrant of the mental efficiency matrix (see chapter 4). Without clear planning, you will not be able to structure your time to focus on anything, and you will live in a mental mess.

Try to take five minutes every morning, before opening your email, to schedule blocks of time for your most important activities. Also be careful to be realistic in your planning, by setting aside time for preparation, travel time, lunch and time for follow-up meetings. When planning your day, make sure to leave one block open for unplanned and emergency issues that will inevitably land on your desk.

Also take fifteen minutes every week to plan ahead, and take the time once a month to make more long term plans. Once you're at it, make sure you plan some time for yourself too.

CBMT PROGRAM, WEEK 6

Mindfulness training: Open attention

Mental strategy # 6: Balance

Our mind has a tendency to evaluate everything and everyone it meets. It divides things into three categories: what it likes, what it dislikes and what it is indifferent to. When the mind is judgmental, it is difficult to be present in the moment. If the mind dislikes something, it puts attention on pushing it away or suppressing it. When it likes something, it uses a lot of energy to cling to it, maintain it or get more of it. In this way, you will easily end up in a constant battle in which you either try to push away or cling to everything you encounter.

During mindfulness training, try to let go of all judgment. Instead of judging, try to be with the circumstances as they are. If something is pleasurable, observe that neutrally without clinging to it. If something is painful, observe it neutrally, but without the desire to get rid of it.

> Free your mind from constantly rejecting certain things and longing for others. Think clearly, without desire for what you do not have, without aversion to what you do have.

Theme # 6: Email with mindfulness

Create some mental space in the email era.

Some facts about how email is used in business:

- 60 per cent check their email when they are on holiday.
- 25 per cent can't manage more than three days without checking their email.
- 50 per cent check their email constantly.
- 70 per cent allow themselves to be distracted by incoming email.

Doctors estimate that around 11 million Americans suffer from "email addiction." A few simple habits can help you create a better overview and mental balance for emailing:

- Turn off all notifications so you don't get distracted by incoming email.
- Set aside some time each day to check and reply to email. Close your email inbox the rest of the time.
- Consider how often you want to email. In most corporate cultures, 2-3 times per day is sufficient.
- Consider which times of the day work best for you. People are usually at their most creative during the first hours of the morning. This can easily be disrupted by 30 minutes of emailing about trivial matters.
- Discuss the email culture of your company with colleagues and employees.
- Email is a quick and easy way to communicate. Unfortunately, there is a risk that it may be too fast. A single word or sentence can be interpreted differently than the intent behind it. A single word, not to mention whole sentences, can cause hours of anger, confusion, worry, doubt, fear and other energy-consuming states of mind. Using a moment of mindfulness before sending an email can save you misunderstandings, time and energy, both individually and collectively.

Every time you write an email, before you send it, take a break and ask yourself:
Does this message need to be sent at all?
Does it contain the message and all the information I want to convey?
How will the recipient perceive this message?

This approach can then be applied to all forms of written communication.

CBMT PROGRAM, WEEK 7

Mindfulness training: Open attention

Mental strategy # 7: Acceptance

You have the freedom to alter many of the circumstances of your life for the better, and this is something you should definitely do. However, there are things that cannot be changed. Acceptance means that you don't make difficult situations worse. You can't always control everything life throws at you, but you can choose how you react.

Acceptance does not mean you have to endure everything that comes your way with passive tolerance. Acceptance is the ability to see life exactly as it is, and not get upset about things you can't change.

> If you can change something, why worry? If you can't change something, why worry?

When you are in an unsatisfactory situation, either make an effort to change it, or accept it as it is. Do not let the feeling of dissatisfaction make matters worse. Do not start an internal fight. In difficult situations, acceptance is often the best strategy in order to deal with stress. When you practice mindfulness, do it with acceptance. Whatever occurs during training, embrace it with acceptance. Expand this attitude of acceptance to include yourself. Accept yourself.

> When you have a problem, change it or let it be, but don't start an internal fight. Don't make it heavy and solid. It is what it is. Accept it with a light-hearted attitude.
> Take it easy, it's good enough.

Theme # 7: Meetings with mindfulness

We have all experienced people who are not present with us. We have also noticed when we are not present with others. The greatest gift you can give someone is your full presence. The essence of practicing mindfulness in meetings is that you are fully present with the people you have in front of you, for as long as you are with them. In this way, all meetings turn into mindfulness training, and the person in front of you becomes the object of your attention.

To be completely present with the people we are with is not just a friendly gesture, it is also a very effective way to get to the point, train our focus, and save time and energy.

There are three phases in all meetings: preparation, the actual meeting and finishing.

- *Preparation:* When you are on the way to a formal meeting, take a mindfulness pause before going into the meeting (three breaths with ABCD). This makes it possible for you to let go of where you have come from and focus on what lies ahead of you. If the corporate culture permits, meetings can begin in this way with all participants.
- *The meeting:* The basic principle is that you are fully present with everyone in the meeting, as long as the meeting lasts. If all parties are fully present with each other and the common agenda, it will save time and energy for everyone. As well as this, everyone will have a more pleasant experience of the meeting.
- *Finishing:* Good meetings can be finished with complete mindfulness, so that they do not take unnecessarily long. Meetings with mindfulness require you to be clear enough to finish them.

The same principles can be used for informal meetings, such as when you meet at the coffee machine, in the hallway, or at your desk.

CBMT PROGRAM WEEK 8

Mindfulness training: Open attention

Mental strategy # 8: Letting go

"Letting go" is simply not holding onto all the thoughts and feelings you experience. We are used to involving ourselves in every thought that arises in our consciousness, instead of letting it go like a bird flying past in the sky. In this way, you often carry around a burden of meaningless thoughts. The attitude of letting go of thoughts rather than get involved in them makes your mind lighter and more flexible, like a computer, that has had its hard drive cleaned.

Make use of the "letting go" attitude during your mindfulness training. Without any doubts or concerns, let go of all the thoughts arising in your mind. If there really was an important idea, it will resurface after the training session.

When you are distracted, let go of the distraction. Also release the thoughts that responded to the distraction. Let go of the desire to be present. Let go of everything— except your attention on your breathing.

The result will be awareness and presence.

Theme # 8: Manage your energy

We have several basic sources of energy. The three that we usually focus on are sleep, food and physical exercise. However, there is a fourth source of energy that can have an even bigger impact on how you feel—your thoughts.

Your brain uses 20 per cent of your energy, even though it comprises only 2 per cent of your body weight. Your thoughts can have a big impact on your energy level, and negative thoughts especially consume a lot of mental and physical energy. As well as this, we know that negative thoughts often have a tendency to create a downward spiral.

However, it is not just negative thoughts that drain your energy. Random, automatic thoughts that appear by themselves have the same effect. Research shows that we feel at our best when our thoughts do not wander, but when we are fully present with what we are doing—whatever that happens to be. A moment of presence feels better than a positive thought.

During the working day, it is rarely the physical challenges that drain your energy. The energy thieves are all the wandering thoughts about what you didn't do properly yesterday, and everything you need to do tomorrow. By training yourself to be fully present, without becoming lost in thought, or starting a chain reaction of thoughts, you open up to a huge source of energy.

Take advantage of this, and good luck with your training!

REFERENCES

Ahlstrom, D. (2010): Innovation and growth: How business contributes to society. Academy of Management. *Perspectives*, August, 10–23.

Allen, M. (2013): The balanced mind: the variability of task-unrelated thoughts predicts error monitoring. *Frontiers in Human Neuroscience*, 7 November.

Anderson, N. B. & Anderson, P. E. (2003): *Emotional longevity: What really determines how long you live*. New York: Viking.

Bach, P. & Hayes, S. C. (2002). The use of acceptance and commitment therapy to prevent the rehospitalization of psychotic patients: A randomized controlled trial. *Journal of Consulting and Clinical Psychology*, 70 (5) 1129–1139.

Bojs, K. (2013): Vetenskapskrönika i Dagens Nyheter, 15 December. http://www.dn.se/nyheter/vetenskap/karin-bojs-skala-for-nobel-medan-skeppet-sjunker.

Boyatzis, R. & McKee, A. (2005): *Resonant leadership: Renewing yourself and connecting with others through mindfulness, hope, and compassion*. Harvard Business School Publishing, e-publication.

Brefczynski-Lewis, J. A. (2007): Neural correlates of attentional expertize in long-term meditation practitioners. *PNAS*, 104 (27) 11483–11488.

Brewer, J. (2011): Meditation experience is associated with differences in default mode network activity and connectivity. *PNAS*, 108 (50) 20254–20259.

Bush, M. (2013): Knowing every breath you take. *New York Times*, 5 January.

Bush, M. (2013): *Working with mindfulness. Research and practice of mindful techniques in organizations*. More than Sound LLC, e-publication.

Campbell, M. (2007): *The stress of leadership*. Center for Creative Leadership, www.ccl.org.

Chang, V. (2004): The effects of a mindfulness-based stress reduction program on stress, mindfulness self-efficacy, and positive states of mind. *Stress and Health*, 20 (3) 141–147.

Chaskalson, M. (2011): *The mindful workplace: Developing resilient individuals and resonant organizations with MBSR*. London: Wiley-Blackwell.

Chiesa, A., & Serretti, A. (2009): Mindfulness-based stress reduction for stress management in healthy people: A review and meta-analysis. *Journal of Alternative and Complementary medicine,* 15 (5) 593–600.

Chopra, M. (2011): *The Equanimous Mind.*

Christensen, C. (2010): How will you measure your life. *Harvard Business Review,* July.

Christoff, K. (2009): Experience sampling during MRI reveals default network and executive system contribution to mind wandering. *PNAS,* 106 (21) 8719–8724.

Coleman, F. (2014): Mindfulness: An ancient skill for thriving in the modern innovation economy. *Huffington Post Business,* 8 April.

Condon, P. (2013): Meditation increases compassionate responses to suffering. *Psychological Science,* 21 August, 223.

Csikszentmihalyi, Mihaly (1996): *Creativity – Flow and the psychology of discovery and invention.* New York: Harper Perennial.

Dabbish, L., Mark, G. & Gonzalez, V. (2011): *Why do I keep interrupting myself?: Environment, habit, and self-interruption.* Vancouver, B.C.: ACM Press. (Proceedings of the twenty-ninth annual SIGCHI conference on human factors in computing systems.)

Dallman, M. (2003): Chronic stress and obesity: A new view of "comfort food." *PNAS,* 100 (20) 11696–11701.

Davenport, T. H. & Beck, J. C. (2001): *The attention economy.* Boston: Harvard Business School Press.

Davidson, R. J & Begley, S. (2012): *The emotional life of your brain. How its unique patterns affect the way you think, feel, and live – and how you can change them.* New York: Hudson Street Press.

Davidson, R. J., & Lutz, A. (2007): Buddha's brain: Neuroplasticity and meditation. *IEEE Signal Process Magazine,* 176, September.

Dhiman, S. (2012): Mindfulness and the art of living creatively: Cultivating a creative life by minding our mind. *Journal of Social Change,* 4 (1) 24–33.

Diestel, S., Cosmar, M. & Schmidt, K. (2013): Burnout and impaired cognitive functioning: The role of executive control in the performance of cognitive tasks. *Work & Stress: An International Journal of Work, Health & Organisations,* 27 (2).

Dolman, E. & Bond, D. (2011): Mindful leadership: Exploring the value of meditation practice. *The Ashridge Journal*, 360 (spring) 36–43.

Drucker, P. F. (2009): *Management challenges for the 21st century*. New York: Harper Collins.

Ekberg, S. (2011): *Stressfri på jobbet*. Bokförlaget Redaktionen. Stockholm.

Ekman, P. (2007): *Emotions revealed: Recognizing faces and feelings to improve communication and emotional life*. New York: Time Books.

Epel, E. (2009): *Can meditation slow rate of cellular aging? Cognitive stress, mindfulness, and telomeres*. San Francisco, CA: University of California San Francisco, Department of Psychiatry.

Farb, N. A. (2010): Minding one's emotions: mindfulness training alters the neural expression of sadness. *Emotion*, 10 (1) 25–33.

Fell, Juergen (2012). I think, therefore I am (unhappy). *Frontiers in Human Neuroscience*, (6), 16 May.

Foerde, K., Knowlton, B. J. & Poldrack, R. A. (2007): Modulation of competing memory systems by distraction. *PNAS*, 103 (31) 11778–11783.

Fox, M. D. (2005): The human brain is intrinsically organized into dynamic, anticorrelated functional. *PNAS*, 102 (27) 9673–9678.

Gareld, J. (2011): *Mindfulness and ethics: Attention, virtue and perfection*. www.smith.edu/philosophy/docs/gareld.

Gaser, C. & Schlaug, G. (2003): Brain structures differ between musicians and non-musicians. *Journal of Neuro- science*, 23 (27) 9240–9245.

George, B. (2012): Mindfulness helps you become a better leader. *Harvard Business Review Blog Network*, 26 October.

Gilbert, P. (2010): *The compassionate mind*. London: Constable & Robinson.

Goldin, P., Ramel, W. & Gross J. (2009): Mindfulness meditation training and self-referential processing in social anxiety disorder: behavioural and neural effects. *Journal of Cognitive Psychotherapy*, 23 (3) 242–257.

Goleman, D. (2013): *Focus: The hidden driver of excellence*. New York: Harper Collins.

Gonzales, Maria (2012): *Mindful leadership: The 9 ways to self-awareness, transforming yourself, and inspiring others*. San Francisco: Jossey-Bass.

Grant, J. (2010): Cortical thickness and pain sensitivity in Zen meditators. *Emotion*, 10 (1) 43–53.

Greenberg, J., Reiner, K. & Meiran, N. (2012): Mind the trap: Mindfulness practice reduces cognitive rigidity. *PLoS ONE*, 15 May.

Grossman, P. (2004): Mindfulness-based stress reduction and health benefits. A meta-analysis. *Journal of Psycho-somatic Research*, (57) 35–43.

Gunaratana, B. (2006): *Mindfulness in plain English*. Somerville, MA: Wisdom Publications.

Hallowell, E. M. (2008): Overload circuits: Why smart people underperform. *Harvard Business Review*, online.

Hanson, R. (2013): *Hardwiring happiness. The new brain science of contentment, calm and condense*. New York: Harmony Books.

Hanson, R. & Mendius, R. (2009): *Buddha's brain. The practical neuroscience of happiness, love, and wisdom*. Oakland: New Harbinger Publications.

Hasenkamp, W. (2012): Mind wandering and attention during focused meditation: A fine-grained temporal analysis of fluctuating cognitive states. *NeuroImage*, 59 (1) 750–760.

Hoffman, G. (2012): How mindfulness can help your creativity. *World of Psychology. Psych Central*, http://psychcentral.com/blog/archives.

Hougaard, R., Carter J. & Coutts G (2015): *One second ahead*. New York: Palgrave Macmillan.

Hunter, J. & Chaskalson, M. (2013): *Making the mindful leader: Cultivating skills for facing adaptive challenges.*

Skipton Leonard, H. (ed.). *The Wiley-Blackwell Handbook of the psychology of leadership, change, and organizational development*. Hoboken: Wiley-Blackwell.

Hölzel, B. K. (2007): Mindfulness practice leads to increases in regional brain gray matter density. P*sychiatry Research: Neuroimaging,* 191 (1) 36–43.

Inglehart, R. & Welzel, C. (2010): The World Value Survey cultural map: Changing mass priorities: The link between modernization and democracy. *Perspectives on Politics,* 8 (2) 551–567.

Is multitasking more efficient? (2001): *APA Online Press Release,* 5 August.

James, W. (1890): *Principles of psychology*. London: MacMillan &Co.

Jha, A. P. (2010): Examining the protective effects of mindfulness training on working memory capacity and affective experience. *Emotion*, 10 (1) 54–64.

Kabat-Zinn, J. (2013): *Full catastrophe living.* Rev. utg. London: Piatkus Books.

Kegan, R. & Lahey, L. (2010): *Immunity to change: How to overcome it and unlock the potential in yourself and your organization.* Cambridge, MA: Harvard Business Press.

Keller, G. & Papasan, Jay (2013): *The one thing. The surprisingly simple truth behind extraordinary results.* London: John Murray.

Keng, S.-L., Smoski, M. J. & Robins, C. J. (2011): Effects of mindfulness on psychological health: a review of empirical studies. *Clinical Psychology Review,* 31 (6) 1041–1056.

Killingsworth, M. A. & Gilbert, D. T. (2010): A wandering mind is an unhappy mind. *Science,* (330) 12 November.

Lally, P. (2009): *How are habits formed: Modelling habit formation in the real world.* Wiley Online Library.

Langer, E. J. (2005): *On becoming an artist: Reinventing yourself through mindful creativity.* New York: Ballantine Books.

Lavallee, C. F., Hunter, M. D. & Persinger, M. A. (2011): Intracerebral source generators characterizing concentrative meditation. *Cognitive Processes,* 12 (2) 141–150.

Lazar, Sara m.. (2005): Meditation experience is associated with increased cortical thickness. Neuroreport, 16 (17) 1893–1897.

Levy, D. M. m.. (2012): The effects of mindfulness meditation training on multitasking in a high-stress information environment. *Proceedings of Graphic Interface,* May.

Mark, G., Gudith, D. & Klocke, U. (2008): *The cost of interrupted work: More speed and stress.* New York: ACM Press.

Meyer, D. E. (1997): A computational theory of executive cognitive processes and multiple-task performance: Part 1. Basic mechanisms. *Psychological Review,* (104) 3–65.

Multitasking is counterproductive (2001): *CNN.com/Career,* 6 December.

Nhat Hanh, T. (2011): *Mindfulness: ögonblickets under.* Stockholm: Lind & Co.

Ophir, E., Nass, C. & Wagner, A. D. (2009): Cognitive control in media multitaskers. *PNAS,* 106 (37) 15583–15587.

Pashler, H. (1992): Attentional limitations in doing two tasks at the same time. *Current Directions in Psychological Science,* 44 (1) 2.

Reb, J., Narayanan, J. & Chaturvedi, S. (2012): Leading mindfully: Two studies on the influence of supervisor trait mindfulness on employee well-being and performance. *Mindfulness,* (2014) (5) 36–45.

Redick, T. S. & Engle, R. W. (2006): Working memory capacity and attention network test performance. *Applied Cognitive Psychology,* 20 (5), 713–721.

Rock, D. (2009): *Your brain at work.* New York: Harper Business.

Rosch, E. (2006): Beginner's mind: Paths to the wisdom that is not learned. I: Ferrari, M. & Potworowski, G. (red.). *Teaching for wisdom.* Hillsdale, NJ: Erlbaum.

Rubinstein, J. S. (2001): Executive control in cognitive processes in task switching. *Journal of Experimental Psychology: Human Perception and Performance,* 27 (4) 763–797.

Santorelli, S. (1999): *Healthy self.* New York: Random House.

Schooler, J. W. (2011): Meta-awareness, perceptual decoupling and the wandering mind. *Trends in Cognitive Science,* 15 (7) 319–326.

Segal, Z. V., Williams, J. M. G. & Teasdale, J. D. (2002): *Mindfulness-based cognitive therapy for depression: A new approach to preventing relapse.* New York: Guilford Press.

Senge, P. (2005): *Presence – An exploration of profound change in people, organizations and society.* New York: Random House.

Shapiro, S. L., Brown, K. W. & Biegel, G. M. (2007): Teaching self-care to caregivers: Effects of mindfulness-based stress reduction on the mental health of therapists in training. *Training and Education in Professional Psychology,* 1 (2) 105–115.

Sood, A. & Jones, D. T (2013): Mind wandering, attention, brain networks and meditation. *EXPLORE,* May/June.

Spaxman, A. (2011): Mindfulness: An antidote to multitasking. *Human Resources,* December.

Ström, M. & Ström, M. (2013): *Effects of corporate based mindfulness training on employee well-being and performance – a pilot study.* Stockholm: Stockholms universitet.

Tan, C.-M. (2012): *Search inside yourself.* New York: Harper Collins.

Tang, Y.-Y. (2010): Short-term meditation induces white matter changes in the anterior cingulate. *PNAS,* 107 (35) 15649–15652.

Treadway, M. T. & Lazar, Sara W. (2009): The neurobiology of mindfulness. Didonna, F. (ed.). *Clinical handbook of mindfulness.* New York: Springer.

Uddin, L. Q. (2009): Functional connectivity of default mode network components: correlation, anticorrelation, and causality. I: *Human Brain Mapping.* New York: Wiley-Liss.

Van Veen, V., & Carter, C. S. (2002): The anterior cingulate as a conflict monitor: fMRI and ERP studies. *Physiology & Behavior,* 77 (4–5) 477–482.

Van Veen, V. & Carter, C. S. (2006): Conflict and cognitive control in the brain. *Current Directions in Psychological Science,* 15 (5) 237–240.

Vgontzas, A. N. (1998): Chronic insomnia and activity of the stress system: a preliminary study. *Journal of Psychosomatic Research,* 45 (1) 21–31.

Wallace, A. B. (2006): *The attention revolution: Unlocking the power of the focused mind.* Boston: Wisdom publications.

Weissman, D. H. m. . (2006): The neural bases of momentary lapses in attention. *Nature Neuroscience,* 9 (7) 971–978.

Wilson, T. D. (2002): *Strangers to ourselves. Discovering the adaptive unconscious.* Cambridge, MA: Belknap.

Woollett, K. & Maguire, E. A. (2011): Acquiring "the Knowledge" of London's layout drives structural brain changes. *Current Biology,* 21 (24–2) 2109–2114.

Yeung, N. & Monsell, S. (2003): Switching between tasks of unequal familiarity: The role of stimulus-attribute and response-set selection. *Journal of Experimental Psychology: Human Perception and Performance,* 29 (2) 455–469.

Zeidan, F. (2010): Mindfulness meditation improves cognition: evidence of brief mental training. *Consciousness and Cognition, (in press).*

MARTIN STRÖM is a leader in the field of corporate mindfulness and senior consultant with Potential Project, the world's top provider of corporate mindfulness since 2010.

Holding master's degrees in computer science and technology as well as psychology, Ström is a regular keynote speaker and trains business leaders in how to implement corporate mindfulness. He has worked with companies such as Accenture, Bain & Company, IKEA, Danone, and PwC.

Ström was responsible for one of the first scientific studies on mindfulness in the workplace, and in 2014, his book Focus at Work was named HR book of the year. He lives with his wife and daughter in Stockholm, Sweden.

SARA HULTMAN works as a writer, psychologist and mindfulness trainer. She has a Masters in Psychology (in cognitive behavioural therapy, CBT, and acceptance and commitment therapy, ACT) and a Bachelor of Journalism. Recently Sara also became a Corporate Based Mindfulness Training (CBMT) trainer with the Potential Project.

Sara mainly works with clients struggling to cope with high demands of modern worklife. She currently lives where the forest meets the water in Stockholm with her two sons, a cat, and a flatmate.

CPSIA information can be obtained
at www.ICGtesting.com
Printed in the USA
LVOW13s1815010617
536600LV00014B/1143/P